First World War
and Army of Occupation
War Diary
France, Belgium and Germany

21 DIVISION
Divisional Troops
Divisional Trench Mortar Batteries
1 March 1916 - 19 December 1918

WO95/2143/3

The Naval & Military Press Ltd
www.nmarchive.com
Published in association with The National Archives

Published by

The Naval & Military Press Ltd

Unit 10 Ridgewood Industrial Park,
Uckfield, East Sussex,
TN22 5QE England
Tel: +44 (0) 1825 749494

www.naval-military-press.com
www.nmarchive.com

This diary has been reprinted in facsimile from the original. Any imperfections are inevitably reproduced and the quality may fall short of modern type and cartographic standards.

© **Crown Copyright**
Images reproduced by permission of The National Archives, London, England, 2015.

Contents

Document type	Place/Title	Date From	Date To
Heading	2143/3 Divisional Trench Mortar Brigade		
Heading	21st Division 21st Trench Mortar Bde Mar 1916-Dec 1918		
Heading	21st Divisional Artillery Late 42nd Trench Mortar Battery X/21 Trench Mortar Battery March To December 1916 (less May & November)		
War Diary	Sheet 36 I 23.D.0.3/1/2	01/03/1916	22/03/1916
War Diary	Rest Camp	23/03/1916	04/04/1916
War Diary	Bissey-Les-Daours	05/04/1916	21/04/1916
War Diary	Map 62d NE2 F.2.b.3.5	22/04/1916	30/04/1916
War Diary	Map 57d S.E.4 X. 26.a	01/06/1916	01/07/1916
War Diary	Map 62d N.E. 2	01/07/1916	25/07/1916
War Diary	Map Lens 11	25/07/1916	31/07/1916
War Diary		01/08/1916	27/08/1916
War Diary	X 21 Trench Mortar Battery	26/09/1916	30/10/1916
Heading	21st Divisional Artillery W/21 Trench Mortars June & July 1916		
War Diary	1/10,000 57.S.E.4	01/06/1916	30/06/1916
War Diary	Map 62d N E 2	01/07/1916	31/07/1916
Heading	21st Divisional Artillery V/21 Heavy Trench Mortars. June To December 1916. Dec 18		
War Diary		01/06/1916	30/06/1916
War Diary	Map 62D N E 2	01/07/1916	31/07/1916
War Diary	(Lens. 6d) G-3.3	01/08/1916	03/08/1916
War Diary	(Lens. 6d) F2-1.3	05/08/1916	14/08/1916
War Diary	(Lens. 6d) J3-2.5	14/08/1916	14/08/1916
War Diary	N.2 Pit 17.c-9.5	14/08/1916	14/08/1916
War Diary	N.2 Pit G.11.D.7 1/2. 8 1/2	14/08/1916	14/08/1916
War Diary	N.1 (17.c 95)	01/09/1916	10/09/1916
War Diary	No.2 (G.11D.7 1/2 8 1/2)	10/09/1916	14/09/1916
War Diary	Sheet 62 C. N. W. a 1 a 1025	15/09/1916	28/09/1916
Heading	21st Divisional Artillery Late 45th Trench Mortar Battery Y/21 Trench Mortar Battery March To December 1916		
War Diary	Sheet 36 NW C16.D.7.6	13/03/1916	22/03/1916
War Diary	Sheet 36 NW C16.D.7.6	01/03/1916	12/03/1916
War Diary	Map 62.D.N.E.2 F2.B.3.5	01/04/1916	30/04/1916
War Diary	Map 62.D.N.E.2 F2.B.3.6	01/05/1916	30/05/1916
War Diary	F2.A.0.1	01/06/1916	30/06/1916
War Diary	Map Manuall 62 D N.E.2	01/07/1916	01/07/1916
War Diary	G.2.B.2.4	01/07/1916	31/07/1916
War Diary	G.17.b.50	01/08/1916	23/08/1916
War Diary	G.17.B.5.0 In The Field	01/09/1916	13/09/1916
War Diary	A27D25	01/10/1916	26/10/1916
War Diary	Map 36c N.W.1 Ref G4.a.9.6	28/10/1916	27/11/1916
War Diary	Map 36c N.W.3 G4.c	28/11/1916	27/12/1916
Heading	21st Divisional Artillery Late 51st Trench Mortar Battery Z/21 Trench Mortar Battery March To December 1916		
Miscellaneous	From O.C. French Mortar Bde	06/07/1916	06/07/1916

Type	Location	Start	End
War Diary	5th Corps Area	01/03/1916	09/03/1916
War Diary	Sheet No 36 N.W.	10/03/1916	10/03/1916
War Diary	C.28.d.3.0	11/03/1916	23/03/1916
War Diary	Borre	23/03/1916	31/03/1916
War Diary	Map 62D N F 2 F.2.B.3.5	01/04/1916	30/04/1916
War Diary	Map 62D N.E.2 F2b 1 1/2 4 1/2	01/05/1916	29/05/1916
War Diary	Map 57 S.E.4 X26b 28	01/06/1916	01/07/1916
War Diary	Map 62D NE2	01/07/1916	31/07/1916
War Diary	Map 51B N.W. 1 A29.b	01/08/1916	26/08/1916
War Diary	Map 51B N.W. 1 Roclincourt A.29.b	27/08/1916	14/09/1916
War Diary	A27D28	01/10/1916	27/10/1916
War Diary	Map N.W.36.C	01/11/1916	26/11/1916
War Diary	Map Loos 36c.N.W.3 G.11.d	01/12/1916	26/12/1916
Miscellaneous		27/01/1917	27/01/1917
War Diary		01/01/1917	29/01/1917
War Diary	Ferfay Worm Houdt	01/02/1917	11/02/1917
War Diary	Battn	11/02/1917	16/02/1917
War Diary	A.27.c 92.80	16/02/1917	28/02/1917
War Diary	Map 36.B.N.E.L.3	01/02/1917	24/02/1917
War Diary		01/03/1917	31/03/1917
War Diary	Cambrin	01/03/1917	05/03/1917
War Diary	Sailly La Borse	06/03/1917	07/03/1917
War Diary	Bethune	07/03/1917	14/03/1917
War Diary	Lucheux	14/03/1917	18/03/1917
War Diary	Arras	22/03/1917	26/03/1917
War Diary	Aolinfer	26/03/1917	31/03/1917
War Diary	G11.d.9.2	01/03/1917	21/03/1917
War Diary	Map Ref France Sheet 51 B.S.W S.29.d	01/04/1917	28/04/1917
War Diary	Map France Sheet 51 B.S.W S.29.d	01/04/1917	30/04/1917
War Diary	S29.d.29	01/05/1917	31/05/1917
War Diary	S29.d.29	01/05/1917	24/05/1917
War Diary	S29.d.29	02/05/1917	24/05/1917
War Diary	S.29.d.2.9	02/05/1917	27/05/1917
War Diary	S.29d.2.9	02/05/1917	31/05/1917
War Diary	S.29.d.2.9	02/05/1917	27/05/1917
War Diary	U.13.a.10.5	16/07/1917	30/07/1917
War Diary			
War Diary	T.18.B.8.2	01/07/1917	31/07/1917
War Diary	T.18.B.8.2	01/07/1917	25/07/1917
War Diary	T.18.B.7.4	01/08/1917	31/08/1917
War Diary	T.18.B.7.4	01/08/1917	14/08/1917
War Diary	(U14)	17/08/1917	30/08/1917
War Diary	T18.B.7.4	06/08/1917	31/08/1917
War Diary	Map Belgium France Sheet 28 H.32.d.5.1	01/09/1917	30/09/1917
War Diary	Sheet 28 H.32.d.5.1		
War Diary	Ref. Map 1/20,000 51.B.N.W. H.I.C 88	01/11/1917	30/03/1918
Heading	21st Divisional Artillery 21st Divisional Trench Mortar Brigade April 1918		
War Diary		01/04/1918	28/07/1918
War Diary	Acheux	26/07/1918	29/08/1918
War Diary	Mailly-Maillet	25/08/1918	27/08/1918
War Diary		01/09/1918	30/09/1918
Heading	War Diary 21st Trench Mortar Brigade RFA October 1st-31st 1918		
War Diary		01/10/1918	29/10/1918

Heading	War Diary Of 21st Trench Mortar Brigade R.F.A. From 1st November 1918 To 30th November 1918		
War Diary		04/11/1918	30/11/1918
Heading	War Diary Of 21st Trench Mortar Brigade. R.F.A. From:- December 1st. To:- December 31st 1918		
War Diary		13/12/1918	19/12/1918

2143/2

Divisional Trench Mortar Brigade

21ST DIVISION

21ST TRENCH MORTAR BDE.
MnK
1916-DEC 1918

21st Divisional Artillery.

Late 42nd Trench Mortar Battery

X/21 TRENCH MORTAR BATTERY

MARCH TO DECEMBER 1916.

(less May & November)

WAR DIARY or INTELLIGENCE SUMMARY.

Army Form C. 2118.

F.2. Ypres Trenches
March 1916

Place	Date	Hour	Summary of Events and Information	Remarks and references to Appendices
Sheet 36 I.23.d.o.3.	1/3/16		No shelling today, but perhaps preparing bombards	
	2/3/16	10.30 a.m.	Got no on following day. Bombardment commenced at 10.30 a.m. Opened with our 2" Emplacement in 68 Trench - fires from trenches 69 & 70 at Enemy saline opposit Nicholson as follows:- Oil Bombs — 30 2" — 22 4" — 27 79	
	2/3/16		The work done was very useful, convenient openings to enemy trenches seemed. The enemy retaliated very vigorously bombard- -ing 15" position. The fires together exploded 30 or firm	

WAR DIARY
or
INTELLIGENCE SUMMARY.
(Erase heading not required.)

Army Form C. 2118.

Place	Date	Hour	Summary of Events and Information	Remarks and references to Appendices
	2/2/16		Sector quiet in during night in the second retaliation – nothing doing.	
	3/2/16		Very heavy snow. Clearing from positions, work on new emplacements very difficult. Continued work on Portugal Redan Emplacement & dugout	
	5/2/16		Also on 2" Portion in Trench 90.	
	6/2/16		General work as per as possible in the weather.	
	7/2/16		Weather again bad – cleared up 15" howitzer in Trench 67. Registered two rounds short by infantry Y.3. Prepared positions for short in Trench Y.3. Continued work on 2" portion in 68.	
	8/2/16		Carried down to Reserve Emplacements. Change over Set for carrying Reserve Emplacement – E & G Guns. Lieut 25-18 [?] Rounds from Trench Y.3. Very useful work on Machine Gun emplacement known as the "Black Redoubt". La Bassée Hamlet.	L.Brown O.C. Y.2 Trench Mortars

Army Form C. 2118.

WAR DIARY
or
INTELLIGENCE SUMMARY.
(Erase heading not required.)

Instructions regarding War Diaries and Intelligence Summaries are contained in F. S. Regs., Part II. and the Staff Manual respectively. Title pages will be prepared in manuscript.

S+/2, T.M. 15
A 2w Infty

Place	Date	Hour	Summary of Events and Information	Remarks and references to Appendices
	10/3/5		Work continued on 2nd replacement Trench 66. Completed dugout in Portugal Reserve.	
	11/3/5	1.30 pm	Replacement. Comm. trench to Trench 73 in use on following day. Repaired position in Trench 73 & relieved by 2 coys Rifle Brigade in front of relaxation. A fire 20 rounds of 18 lb (short-fuzed) on Railway Saline against wire & parapet with excellent result (burst = duds)	
	12/3/5		Proceeded with 2nd replacement Trench 68, also cleared up front-line & lift bnse. Also general work.	
	13/3/5		Worked my sect. carried on general work, cleaning up frontwire etc.	
	14/3/5		Our raided plain Bomb-Store Lothian Avenue cleaned & refilled bombs.	
	15/3/5		Repaired 2nd position Trench 73. carried bombs to top trench for use in following 2 days.	
	16/3/5		Fired 4 Heavy round + 5° dropper (kingtailed) with good results. The German retaliation not severe.	
	17/3/5		General work carried on as usual.	
	18/3/5		Work completed Portugal Reserve.	
	19/3/5		Cleared trench over Portugal Reserve Supplement, rifle trench & cleaned 18 pm.	

T2134. Wt. W708—776. 500000. 4/15. Sir J. C. & 8.

Army Form C. 2118.

X/21 T.M. B'y

WAR DIARY
or
INTELLIGENCE SUMMARY.
(Erase heading not required.)

Instructions regarding War Diaries and Intelligence Summaries are contained in F. S. Regs., Part II. and the Staff Manual respectively. Title pages will be prepared in manuscript.

Date	Hour	Summary of Events and Information	Remarks and references to Appendices
1915 Dec 31 20/3/16		Cleared position to gun Trench 70 also cleared dug-outs Mountain Bty position in Rotten Avenue.	
21/3/16		Took big Oxygen & oil pan & tools etc. Cleared all dug outs etc.	
22/3/16		Handed over Tripple to new 17th Division who arrived at 4.0 pm.	
23/3/16		Proceeded to Rue Camp no horse by Motor mule lorries, arriving about 3.30 pm.	
24/3/16		General fatigues, cleaning billets &c.	
25/3/16		Foot-ball route march in morning.	
26/3/16		2/Lt J.S. Stowie took over command from Lt. Braen. Physical drill, Machine drill, & Route March. Church Parade.	
27/3/16		Physical Drill & Gun drill.	
28/3/16		Gun march.	
29/3/16		" "	
30/3/16		" "	
31/3/16		Marched to Carol, entrained & proceeded to Busary the Dacurs.	

J.S. Stowie 2/Lt R.F.A.
O/C X/21 T.M. B'y

#21 Trench Mortar Battery

April 1916

Army Form C. 2118.

WAR DIARY
or
INTELLIGENCE SUMMARY.
(Erase heading not required.)

Instructions regarding War Diaries and Intelligence Summaries are contained in F. S. Regs., Part II. and the Staff Manual respectively. Title pages will be prepared in manuscript.

Place	Date	Hour	Summary of Events and Information	Remarks and references to Appendices
Busnes-les-Jeauves	1/4/16			
	2/4/16			
	3/4/16		Battery at rest.	
	4/4/16			
	5/4/16			
	6/4/16			
	7/4/16		Arrived Meaulte.	
	8/4/16		General fatigues + cleaning billets.	
	9/4/16			
	10/4/16		Down in trenches. Started making Emplacements.	
	11/4/16			
	12/4/16		Building 2" Emplacements	
	13/4/16		" "	
	14/4/16		" "	
	15/4/16		" "	
	16/4/16		" "	

J. Jones 2/Lt. R.F.A.
O/C 1/21 T.M.B.

Army Form C. 2118.

WAR DIARY
or
INTELLIGENCE SUMMARY.
(Erase heading not required.)

4/21 Trench Mortar By.

April 1916

Instructions regarding War Diaries and Intelligence Summaries are contained in F. S. Regs., Part II. and the Staff Manual respectively. Title pages will be prepared in manuscript.

Place	Date	Hour	Summary of Events and Information	Remarks and references to Appendices
	17/4/16		Building emplacements. Returned to billets evening.	
	18/4/16		Went to I. Army Trench Mortar School.	
	19/4/16		Course in firing Trench mortars.	
	20/4/16		Instruction in 2" pin Ammunition etc.	
	21/4/16		Returned to billets.	
Map 52A NE 22 4/16	22/4/16		Building emplacements & translating in Trenches.	
A2 6. 3. 5.	23/4/16		"	
	24/4/16		"	
	25/4/16		"	
	26/4/16		"	
	27/4/16		"	
	28/4/16		"	
	29/4/16		"	
	30/4/16		"	

J. Stevens 2 Lt R.F.A.
O/C 4/21 T.M.B.

Army Form C. 2118.

X 21 Trench Mortar Battery.

Vol /2

WAR DIARY
or
INTELLIGENCE SUMMARY.
(Erase heading not required.)

Instructions regarding War Diaries and Intelligence Summaries are contained in F.S. Regs., Part II. and the Staff Manual respectively. Title pages will be prepared in manuscript.

Place	Date	Hour	Summary of Events and Information	Remarks and references to Appendices
Map 57D S.E.4 X.26.a.	June 1st to 7th		Battery resting	
	June 7th to 23rd		Battery fired 105 rounds retaliation to German Minnenwerfer. The shooting was always effective and succeeded in silencing the hostile Trench Mortars. Work was at the same time carried out on emplacements, four new ones being dug in this period including a bombstore for each gun position.	

W.Y. Robertson 2 Lieut Connaught Rangers
O.C. X 21 Trench Mortar Battery

WAR DIARY or INTELLIGENCE SUMMARY.

Army Form C. 2118.

X 21 Trench Mortar Battery

Place	Date	Hour	Summary of Events and Information	Remarks and references to Appendices
Moq. 57d S.E.a X.26.a.	June 24	4 a.m.	In accordance with orders the battery was in action at 4 a.m. and throughout the day was occupied in cutting enemy wire. Newton fuses were used and heard very effective. 232 rounds were fired and several large breaches were made in the enemy wire from X.26.f.85.70 to X.26.d.78. One per cent were "blinds". Retaliation was very heavy and one man was killed.	
	25	4 a.m.	303 rounds were fired. More breaches were effected and the former gaps considerably widened.	
	26	4 a.m.	51 rounds were fired and wire again damaged. The Germans made no attempt to repair the damage.	
	27	4 a.m.	116 rounds were fired. After this shoot very little wire was left. Retaliation was very heavy but no casualties were caused.	
	28	4 a.m.	87 rounds fired.	
	29	4 a.m.	57 rounds fired.	
	30	4 a.m.	120 rounds fired. German wire completely demolished during general bombardment fired 50 rounds at German trenches. Retaliation extremely heavy. 2 Lieut Horning wounded.	
	July 1st			W.G. Robertson 2/Lieut O.C. X 21 Trench Mortar Battery

WAR DIARY
or
INTELLIGENCE SUMMARY   X.21 Trench Mortar Battery

Army Form C. 2118.

(Erase heading not required.)

Place	Date	Hour	Summary of Events and Information	Remarks and references to Appendices
Map 12 NE.2	July 1st to 20th		Battery in rest billets at E.17.c.	
—Ditto—	21st		Battery lent to 33rd Division. Proceeded with guns and ammunition to F.4.c. but services were not required.	
—Ditto—	21st to 28th		Battery in rest billets at E.17.c.	
Map. LENS.11	25th to 31st		Battery marched to Aoxenu-le-Comte (M.R.3.G.)	

W.G. Robertson, 2 Lieut
Comdg. X.21 French Mortar Battery

WAR DIARY
or
INTELLIGENCE SUMMARY.
(Erase heading not required.)

Army Form C. 2118.

X/4 Folio 1 Vol 4

Place	Date	Hour	Summary of Events and Information	Remarks and references to Appendices
August 1916			X.21 Battery H.Q. On August 3rd Stood over K.1 Section and the left of 7 from the outgoing Division (L'14 Battery). The German Artillery and Trench Mortars shewed little activity at the beginning of August. X.21 Battery retaliates heavily on the enemy's front line and Cmn. Trenches, for every Minenwerfer the increased the number of Minenwerfer fired into our lines, but the Battery always fired the last shot in retaliation. Enemy French Mortars generally quiet during the day, up to 5 or 6 pm when they invariably commenced firing until suppressed. August 17th "November" Avenue "East – Decker – demolished on Enemy Trench Mortar position one after a large endeavour to blow it up. For a week after this rather less Minen appeared to be fired against us, but about this time the Germans commenced sniping with 7.7 cm shell and occasionally 4.2"	

Army Form C. 2118.

folio 2

WAR DIARY
or
INTELLIGENCE SUMMARY.
(Erase heading not required.)

Instructions regarding War Diaries and Intelligence Summaries are contained in F. S. Regs., Part II. and the Staff Manual respectively. Title pages will be prepared in manuscript.

Place	Date	Hour	Summary of Events and Information	Remarks and references to Appendices
August 1916 (continued)			L.21 Battery T.M.B (Continued) of clay and earth (3 to 5 feet high) – 3 in number – were observed along the line of enemy trench which runs North/South parallel with the road at Chanteclar – S.12 a 10/6 to 10/10. This target is out of range for 2" French Mortars. On 23rd and 24th August, as ordered, wire cutting was carried out against enemy Front Line at S/12 a 55.95. The officer who was to use the lanes made expressed himself satisfied with the wire-cutting. On the night of the 23rd August Chanteclar enemy Front Line was bombarded by S.21 Battery simultaneously with the Artillery for 20 minutes. On 25th August the flanks of the point of entry there were had been cut as abovementioned – were similarly bombarded for 20 mts. Korad Shepherd Lieut RFA O.C. S.21 Battery French Mortar Brigade	
Waterloo Street Arquies August 27th 1916				

Army Form C. 2118.

WAR DIARY
or
INTELLIGENCE SUMMARY.
(Erase heading not required.)

Place	Date	Hour	Summary of Events and Information	Remarks and references to Appendices
X.21 Trench Mortar Battery	September 1916.		At the beginning of the month X.21 Battery was in action in Lens & Lièvin sectors of the Divisional Front. On the 3rd the Battery handed over its positions to Z.21 Battery and the personnel proceeded to Third Army Trench Mortar School for a weeks Course, during which the working of the Temple Silencer was expounded. On the 11th the Battery rejoined the Trench Mortar Brigade which was then en route for the Somme Front. Arriving on the Somme Front with the Brigade on the 13th, X.21 Battery was employed till the end of the month on Ordinary fatigues. 26th Sept. 1916. R Sheppard Captain. O.C. X.21 Battery.	

WAR DIARY or INTELLIGENCE SUMMARY

Army Form C. 2118.

Vol 4

Place	Date	Hour	Summary of Events and Information	Remarks and references to Appendices
	October 1916		E.21 Trench Mortar Battery. During the first fortnight of October the Battery did not go into action. The Battery underwent various fatigues. Fatigues were supplied on road-making and subsequently fatigues dug gun-pits on the line taken up by our Field Guns between Hers and Hyl Trone. This area was cleared of timber. Engineers were one of the fatigue parties who quarters were also cleared. The Battery have a number of ammunition dumps placed. The enemy dug with 8" shell trials manoeuvre for positions close to the gun-pits being dug. Moving to another part of the line on Fire Bays march the Battery arrives in its present billeting area. 21st October and relieves outgoing Battery following day. On the front at present vicinity D.21. The enemy has so far been quiet. He employs only Minenwerfer and snipers at present. Our Battery has been observing two Trenchmortars and has cut wire to E.9b (North) of Hairpin Crater. Number appears that the enemy is reluctant to retaliate – even though his Minenwerfer are inflicting enough when receiving fire. He has been searching for the	

WAR DIARY
or
INTELLIGENCE SUMMARY.
(Erase heading not required.)

Army Form C. 2118.

Place	Date	Hour	Summary of Events and Information	Remarks and references to Appendices
	27th October 1916		Stanfield Trench Guns and Trenches Stokes Guns which have been shooting pine tenements into Medicine Avenue fire on the Corners of Rex Avenue and Stanfield Knee. This corner is the circulation feeding the trenches out to the top. In two places with successive shots. He is likely to expect the precis elsewhere. His guns to fire but this does not prevent the Battery cutting this wire or knowing the trench. Stoppages into the air. A sniper that was worrying the Infantry at night has been silenced during the last 3 days. This is ambulance to our firing a couple of rounds of smokeless trench mortars the angle of this spot. R. Hughes Lieut Comdg 221 S.M. Bty	

WAR DIARY
or
INTELLIGENCE SUMMARY.
(Erase heading not required.)

Army Form C.2118.

X/21 Trench Mortar Battery

Vol 6

Place	Date	Hour	Summary of Events and Information	Remarks and references to Appendices
X.21 Trench Mortar Battery	December 1916		During the first half of the month the usual exchange of T.M. fire took place. About the middle of the month the enemy used 7.7mm and 5.9" guns against us, but no more than equalled by our Artillery. On the 22nd December the enemy carried out a bombardment of our front. An attack was expected and prepared for. The enemy, however, did not attack and subsequent orders indicated it was no longer anticipated. X.21 Battery had all guns ready and a free supply of ammunition on hand, and fortified the German front line whilst awaiting the enemy, ready to shorten range when necessary. Sixty weather prevented the Germans many gas, and deep mud both in the trenches and the soft state of the ground in the open would have rendered an attack difficult. Since the 22nd the enemy fires occasional series of 4.2" shell each day as emerges but fires altogether only a fraction of what our own Artillery are putting over. A new projectile has made its appearance. First noticed on the	

Army Form C. 2118. 2

WAR DIARY
or
INTELLIGENCE SUMMARY.
(Erase heading not required.)

Instructions regarding War Diaries and Intelligence Summaries are contained in F. S. Regs., Part II. and the Staff Manual respectively. Title pages will be prepared in manuscript.

Place	Date	Hour	Summary of Events and Information	Remarks and references to Appendices
"Reserve Line"	30th Decem 1916		2pm. It is rather less powerful than the "rescuer" and on account of its high angle is usually fired from a T.M. emplacement. By its very sharp sounding burst and penetrative effects it is evidently a large form of STOKES, and must carry a large proportion of explosive in its total weight. It being twice as fast as the "Minny" in series of up to half a dozen to fire rounds. Accuracy of fire about the same as the "Minny."	F. Shippam 2nd Lt. Comdg 30/21 T.M. Battery.

A   21st Divisional Artillery.

W/21 TRENCH MORTARS

JUNE & JULY 1916.

WAR DIARY
or
INTELLIGENCE SUMMARY.
(Erase heading not required.)

Army Form C. 2118.

Place	Date	Hour	Summary of Events and Information	Remarks and references to Appendices
1/10000 57.S.E.4	June 1916		The Battery was in action on the Trenches from 20th June to 2nd July. Gun Positions were: X 26 a 3.3 "Quickfire", X 26 a 3.5 "102" & "Shrew", X 26 a 3.5 "104" & "Shrew", X 26 a 3.5 "No 4 Mortar", X 26 a 3.10 & "Shrew". Targets: The wire entanglements before Enemy's front line trenches from point X 26 a 8.7 to point X 27 c 4.0. Fact. 40 bombers and Cut wire entanglements preparatory to Infantry advance. Number of rounds fired: 1163. The task was successfully carried out. Casualties: Killed one man. Wounded one Officer, three NCO's and five men.	

R. Huffey Lieut RMA
O.C. V.3.L. Battery
Méaulte 5th July 1916

Army Form C. 2118

WAR DIARY or INTELLIGENCE SUMMARY

(Erase heading not required.)

July 1916
W/21 Medium Trench Mortar Battery

Vol I

Instructions regarding War Diaries and Intelligence Summaries are contained in F. S. Regs., Part II. and the Staff Manual respectively. Title Pages will be prepared in manuscript.

Place	Date 1916	Hour	Summary of Events and Information	Remarks and references to Appendices
Map. 62D.NE2	July 1st to 15th		Battery in rest at Billets at E.19.c.	
	16th		Battery assisted to get 2" Trench Mortar Guns and Ammunition in action in Mametz Wood.	
	17th to 20th		Battery resting in Billets	
	21st		Battery lent to 33rd Division & proceeded with guns and ammunition to Bazentin Wood, but services were not required.	
	22nd		Resting in Billets.	
	24th to 25th		Battery made two journeys to bring guns and ammunition back.	
	26th to 28th		On line of march.	
	29th to 31st		Resting in Billets.	

J H Fiddin
Lieut Gords
p.r. O.C. W.21. Medium Trench Mortar Bty

21st Divisional Artillery.

V/21 HEAVY TRENCH MORTARS.

JUNE to DECEMBER 1916.

Dec '18

WAR DIARY
or
INTELLIGENCE SUMMARY.
(Erase heading not required.)

Army Form C. 2118.

V/21. Heavy Trench Mortar Battery

Vol 1

Place	Date	Hour	Summary of Events and Information	Remarks and references to Appendices
	1-6-16 to 20-6-16		Digging gun positions. Ratio - Battery in the alft working 8 hours a day each. Position for two guns at F.2.d.9.7 shooting on FRICOURT. Position for two guns X.26.c.50.95. OP. at X.25.b.95 + F.8.d.3.7. Reference sheet 57D.S.E 4 + 6 or D.N.E.2	
	21-6-16			
	22-6-16		One French gun arrived to take up position F.2.d.9.7.	
	24-6-16	3.30 a.m.	Bombardment commenced. Battery did not shoot. Two men split gun and shoot. Battery did not shoot. One taken to end firstin came up at night. One taken to end first in	
	25-6-16		Going - Bombardment Fired 23 rounds	
	26.		Fired 24 rounds	
	27		" 70 "	
	28		" 37 "	
	29		" 42 "	
	30		Casualties. One man wounded.	
	"			

J.W. mar
Capt R.F.A
O.C. 21 H.T.M. Battery

21 July

Army Form C. 2118

WAR DIARY
or
INTELLIGENCE SUMMARY

(Erase heading not required.)

V/21 Heavy Trench Mortar Battery.

July 1916.

Instructions regarding War Diaries and Intelligence Summaries are contained in F. S. Regs., Part II. and the Staff Manual respectively. Title Pages will be prepared in manuscript.

Place	Date 1916	Hour	Summary of Events and Information	Remarks and references to Appendices
Map 62D.N.E.2	July 1st to 15th		Resting in Billets. Part Battery with guns in position but inactive, and part in billets. Position of two guns X.26.C.50.95. and one 7.2.d.97.	
	16th		Battery ordered to get Mediums Guns and Ammunition into action in Mametz Wood.	
	17th		Resting in Billets.	
	18th to 25th		Attached to 21st Divisional Artillery Column as a working party on Ammunition Dump	
	26th to 29th		On line of march.	
	29th to 31st		Resting in Billets.	

J J Dudley
Lieut Somers.
O.C. V/21 Heavy Trench Mortar By.

Army Form C. 2118.

1st Heavy Trench Mortar Bty. Vol 2

WAR DIARY
or
INTELLIGENCE SUMMARY

(Erase heading not required.)

For August 1916.

Instructions regarding War Diaries and Intelligence Summaries are contained in F. S. Regs., Part II. and the Staff Manual respectively. Title Pages will be prepared in manuscript.

Place	Date	Hour	Summary of Events and Information	Remarks and references to Appendices
(Sheet 6d) Q.3.3.	1st - 3rd.		The Battery was on the line of march from 1st till the night of 3rd. We then occupied billets and proceeded on 5th to "School of Mortars" for a course of instruction, leaving	
(Sheet 6d) J².1.3.	5th - 14th		there on 14th and returning to billets on the same night.	
(Sheet 6d) J³.2.5.	14th.			
M² Bt. 17.c.9.5.			The Battery commenced digging gun-emplacements on 16th and are still working on the same.	
N² Bt. 9.11.D.7½.8½.				

J. F. Ridler McDowell
Capt ad/ 1st H.T.M.B.
Comdg 1st H.T.M.B.

V/21. Heavy Trench Mortar Bty.

Army Form C.2118.

WAR DIARY
or
INTELLIGENCE SUMMARY

(Erase heading not required.)

For September 1916

Place	Date	Hour	Summary of Events and Information	Remarks and references to Appendices
17.c.95.	1st till 10th		Battery digging Gun Emplacements.	
9.11.D.7½.8½	10th till 14th		On the line of march	
Chied 62.N(a) A.1a 10 25.	15th		Fatigues.	

D. H. Fidler
Capt. R.F.A.
Comdg. V/21. H.T.M.B.

Army Form C. 2118.

WAR DIARY
or
INTELLIGENCE SUMMARY.
(Erase heading not required.)

For October
2/21 Heavy Trench Mortar Bty

Instructions regarding War Diaries and Intelligence Summaries are contained in F. S. Regs., Part II. and the Staff Manual respectively. Title pages will be prepared in manuscript.

Place	Date	Hour	Summary of Events and Information	Remarks and references to Appendices
Sheet N°62.	From 1st till 14th		The Battery was on fatigues for Field Batteries of 94th and 95th Bde	
C. NUV.	15th		Proceeded on the line of march.	
a.10.10.25	21st till 28th		Arrived at destination and took over 3 gun pits. (a27c6.8) (a27c9.6) (g.u.a.9.9.k.5) (a.1.a.10.25). One half of the Battery remaining in Bellili at	

J.F.Dudley.
Lt RFA.
Comdg 2/21 H.T.M.B.

WAR DIARY or INTELLIGENCE SUMMARY

21 D T M B 6
Army Form C. 2118.

For November 1916.

Vol 5

21. H.T.M.B.G.

During the period of this report the guns have been shot regularly on enemy targets according to pre-arranged programme with 2 breaks after referred to. A great deal of good work has been effected in the destruction of enemy trenches and strong points; and generally speaking we have asserted a superiority over enemy Trench Mortars both in damage of activity and in material effect. 310 rounds have been fitted by an average of 75 per shooting of any day.

There have been 5 shoots and 2 duds. The areas affected by the rounds have been A.22; A.27; B.25; Object of the shooting have been almost entirely the destruction of material, 5 enemy personnel are known to have been killed, two bodies being seen and no doubt there were further casualties. From one of the bodies valuable information was obtained on _____. This was referred to in the First Army Intelligence Report for that day + small bomb stores have been blown up on the 13/11/16 an important shoot was carried out in the Cambrian Sector in conjunction with 21st Medium T.M.S. + 5th Div. G.T.M.S. and very good results were obtained. There has been very little retaliation to our shooting and attempted retaliation has been several times silenced. The only casualty in the Battery during this period has been one man wounded on 26/11/16. Two interruptions have occurred to shooting first from 11th to 15th in the Cambrian Sector, where, owing to bad weather, the gun pits and trench apparatus were seriously affected + had to be built up. 2nd 3 days cease firing was ordered pending an investigation into the quality of the cordite charge used for the guns. The night firing has been carried out in the change of the flashes giving the gun positions away + the difficulty of observation has been the more owing to the lack of telephonists and the breakdown of wire. This is now much enforced. In General there has been marked enemy activity in this area. Our activity especially in Artillery T.M.S + Bombs trouble being much greater.

The shoots in this area were as usual Each canadian and gave the impression that little or no work has been done to them by previous divisions. The not working parts there have been overhauled in many places but merely a great deal of work has been carried on and the trenches improved.

The shooting of the Battery has been hampered at times owing to the lack of telephonists but still be enforced.

J. B. Fiddler Lt.

WAR DIARY
or
INTELLIGENCE SUMMARY.
(Erase heading not required.)

Army Form C. 2118.

Place	Date	Hour	Summary of Events and Information	Remarks and references to Appendices
	November 1916		221 Trench Mortar Battery. During the month 221 Battery fired into the enemy's lines from Schwaben and Quadra Salient. We cut the enemy's wire and Blazer in his trenches, wire was extensively cut about 95 c 6/2. 7/2. 9/2. 95 c 3/3 and quantities of bombs dropped into his front line, and into his Communication trenches 75 c 55/25 and 75/20. The enemy has so far fired very little in immediate retaliation to our shooting, but sometimes sends severe dark-small TM's of about 5 lbs. On the 22 inst at 2.30 p.m. we fired 68 rounds in cooperation with Stokes and Artillery. During this "shoot" the enemy did not return a single shot on our Battery front, while our bombs were falling two and three at a time into his trenches at Mouquet Point.	
	24/11/1916		R. M. Moore Lieut RFA Comdn. 221 T.M. Battery	

WAR DIARY or INTELLIGENCE SUMMARY

Army Form C. 2118.

For December, 1916.

Place	Date	Hour	Summary of Events and Information	Remarks and references to Appendices

During the month of December the Left Section Guns in the Stronghorn Sector has been shelled regularly according to arranged Programmes except on the 14th & 16th when there was no firing owing to repairs to Gun Pit by R.E. and laying out a new wire to the O.P. A great deal of damage has been done to enemy trenches, I.M. Positions etc, the area mostly affected being Q5 & Q4.

The 3 guns (A B & C) in the Cambrin Section were handed over on the 8th to W6. H.T.M. Bty after much good shooting had been obtained from them. In particular on 5th Dec. "B" & "C" guns in co-operation with Artillery bombarded "Rifleman Keep" and fired 31 effective shots. On the 1st December "A" Gun fired 15 rounds on Madagascar trench, causing the explosion of a small ammunition dump.

There has been moderate enemy retaliation but no casualties in this Battery during the month. The work of building another emplacement at Q. has been carried on regularly from about the middle of the month. The Heavy T.M. which was stored at Tommelles was on the 8th. handed over to the 24th Divi. H.T.M. Bty. During the month 226 rounds have been fired. Enemy T.M's. are well held in the Cambrin Sector but are very active in

Stronghorn Sector and more shoots "upon these should be carried out."

[signature] for Capt R.F.A.
Commndg 1/2/3 Div.T.M.By.

21st Divisional Artillery.

Late 45th Trench Mortar Battery

Y/21 TRENCH MORTAR BATTERY

MARCH TO DECEMBER 1916.

WAR DIARY or INTELLIGENCE SUMMARY

Army Form C. 2118.

Y/21 Battery
Trench Mortar 73rd

Place	Date	Hour	Summary of Events and Information	Remarks and references to Appendices
Sheet 36 NW C.19.d.7.6	13/3/16		40 rounds 20 L/B + 2 shrap near from k.1 gun at enemy's alarm posts & the front line. front heavily damaged.	
	14/3/16		7 rounds from K.2" gun from T88 retaliation.	
	16/3/16		The enemy retaliating but on other parts of the line.	
			1.48 rounds new gun to 1.2 pm. Steady rate of fire & 1 round per K.2 gun at a O'clock.	
	17/3/16		Firing steady. Enemy quiet.	
	18/3/16		14 rounds of 2" how. from a retaliation to enemy trench mortar. There were small calibre.	
	19/3/16	1920	Not of new enemy trench mortar.	
	21/3/16		9 rounds new gun from K.2" front at request of infantry as a calm sabotage infantry. Brigade were appears to be fire directed here in retaliation.	
	22/3/16		The battery was later out of action.	

M. & R. 21st January
C/Nelson Lt
O.C. Y/21 Battery

Y 21 Battery Trench Army Form C. 2118.

Late A.S.D. Dublin

WAR DIARY
or
INTELLIGENCE SUMMARY.
(Erase heading not required.)

Place	Date	Hour	Summary of Events and Information	Remarks and references to Appendices
Sheet 36 N.W. C.16.D.7.6.	1/3/16		Enemy trenches were fired at with R–1½ gun shrap. H.Ex.y + common. Considerable damage was caused by the former which were fired. 20 rounds light + 20 rounds heavy.	
	2/3/16	3 p.m.	The above target was engaged again during the afternoon. 26 rounds of light 1½ pr shrapnel were fired + further damage was done to the parapet + wire + front.	
	3/3/16		Another section of the enemy trench was was engaged. About 77 R + 20 rounds of heavy 1½ were fired amounted damage was caused to enemy retaliation.	
	4–8·" 3/3/16		Kept our cannon on R recent emplacement + spell firing position on the fire. Nr slain.	
	9/3/16		24 rounds were shelled at a certain farm where enemy's supposed to be till G.O.P. gun field was made. During the shoot 24 rounds were fired from K.1 gun. At the times enemy supposed were seen in front on fresh covered trenches and machine guns fresh dug trenches near Canton	
	10–11·" 3/3/16			
	12/3/16		13 rounds of 2" trench mortars and successfully placed long Boort Trench. Noted with a direct hit.	

Nicholson Major
at Battery

WAR DIARY
or
INTELLIGENCE SUMMARY
(Erase heading not required).

Army Form C. 2118.

Y/21.st Medium Trench Mortar Batt. (2" guns)
April 30th 1916.

Place	Date	Hour	Summary of Events and Information	Remarks and references to Appendices
Map. 62.D.N.E.2.	1–5th		Batty in rest billets	
	8th		Ranging rounds on taking over	
	9th		Improving emplacement	
	10th		" "	
	11th		" "	
	12th			
	13th		Carrying ammunition & work on emplacements	
	15th			
	16th			
	17th			
'F.2.B.3.5.	19th		Batty went to Trench Mortar School	
	20th			
	21st			
	22nd		Fired 12	
	23rd		Fired 14	
	24th		Work on emplacement.	
	25th		Fired 25"	
	26th		26	
	27th		38	
	28th		28	
	29th		74	
	30th		40	

This is not intended of retaliation or opening the enemy's but purely to enable own Batteries to open fire or ranging for future emergency.

All fire carried out under orders of grouped 2nd Lt S.H. Skinn S.H. Son. L.T.
For O.C. Y/21 Trench Mortar Batty.

Army Form C. 2118.

WAR DIARY
or
INTELLIGENCE SUMMARY

(Erase heading not required.) V/21 Trench Mortar Battery

Place	Date	Hour	Summary of Events and Information	Remarks and references to Appendices
Trenches D.W.E. 22.6.3.6.	May 1st		Battery went into trenches with four guns in action against Boche. Thirty rounds were fired in retaliation to Minnenwerfer & rifle grenades.	
	2nd		46 Rounds fired in retaliation (as day before)	
	3rd		39 " " " " as day before	
	4th 5th 6th 7th 8th 9th 10th		Battery in billets. Working parties to trenches daily	
	11th 12th 13th 14th 15th 16th 17th		Battery in trenches. During this period much fighting was done both day & night mostly in retaliation to Boche fire. Some successful work was done and the enemies trenches & works suffered considerable damage. Fired during this period 258. Rounds	

E. David Capt
O.C. V/21 T.M.Bgr.

WAR DIARY
or
INTELLIGENCE SUMMARY

(Erase heading not required.) Y/21 Trench Mortar Battery

Army Form C. 2118.

Place	Date	Hour	Summary of Events and Information	Remarks and references to Appendices
Mars 2nd	May 17th 18th 19th 20th 21st 22nd 23rd 24th 25th 26th 27th 28th 29th 30th		The battery came out of action went to Busay-les-Daours to rest billets	

E. Davoliafi
Capt
Y/21 T.M.By.

Army Form C. 2118.

WAR DIARY
or
INTELLIGENCE SUMMARY.
(Erase heading not required.)

Y2. Trench Mortar Batty.
6.7.16. Vol 8

Place	Date	Hour	Summary of Events and Information	Remarks and references to Appendices
F.2.A.O.1			1 - 30 June 1916.	
	1st	}	Batty in trench. Fired 410 rounds in whole front preparation	
	6.11.a	}	of during Raid on Wickel Corner.	
	11.a	}	Batty out in billets.	
	6.21.a 22	}		
	23		Batty in line. Fired 20 rounds in retaliation & for ranges	
	24		First day of Bombardment. 220 Rounds. ⎫ During the bom-
	25		2nd " " 200 Rounds. ⎬ we lost no guns
	26		3rd " " 160 Rounds. ⎬ blown up & both
	27		4th " " 120 Rounds. ⎬ lost four days
	28		5th " " 64 Rounds ⎬ Several guns were temp-
	29		6th " " 62 Rounds ⎬ out of action.
	30		7th " " 45 rounds. ⎭
			The charges used were found to vary very much you could	
			never be certain whether the Bomb dropped short or no. This was	
			not due to dampness. The Batty lost 3 men killed Lieut Ashton	
			wounded & four men with still shock & one gun destroyed	
			S.H. Stevens 2nd Lt. O.C. Y2 Trench Mortar Batty.	

WAR DIARY or **INTELLIGENCE SUMMARY** Y/21 Trench Mortar Batty July 1916. Army Form C. 2118.

Vol 0

Place	Date	Hour	Summary of Events and Information	Remarks and references to Appendices
Maricourt 62°NE2	1st	6.25 – 7.30 AM	Fired 35 rounds in final bombardment as covering fire of first kind.	
F 2 B 2 4		10.30 AM	Lieut Addena R.F.A. fired two rounds from an advanced position in the German support line having advanced with our gun teams to fire the shots by a tracting party from Faviere. The gun was retaken later in the day.	
	2nd – 3rd		Batty not in action either in rear trenches or at the front.	

G.M. Phillips Lt.
OC Y/21 Trench Mortar B.T.

Army Form C. 2118.

WAR DIARY
or
INTELLIGENCE SUMMARY.

Vol 10
Y/21 Trench Mortar Battery
For Agst 1916.

Place	Date	Hour	Summary of Events and Information	Remarks and references to Appendices
G.17.b.50	August			
	1st 2		Battery in Rest Billets.	
	3rd		Relieved 9th Division	
	7th		Fired three rounds in retaliation	
	10th		Fired two rounds for registration	
	13th		Fired 33 (2 inch) + 7 (1½ inch) rounds.	
	16th		Fired 20 (2 inch bombs) in retaliation	
	17th		Fired 15 (2 inch) and 10 (1½ inch)	
	18th		Fired 49 (2 inch) and 9 (1½ inch)	
	19th		Fired 4 (1½ inch) and 5 (2 inch) bombs.	
	22nd		Fired 31 (2 inch) and 24 (1½ inch).	
	23rd		Fired 46. 2 inch bombs.	

The remainder of the time was spent in digging Gun pits — three being finished and three are at present under construction.

D Vaughan 2nd Lt R.F.A.
O.C. Y/21 T.M.B.

September 1916.

Army Form C. 2118.

WAR DIARY
or
INTELLIGENCE SUMMARY.

Y/21 Trench Mortar Battery

(Erase heading not required.)

Instructions regarding War Diaries and Intelligence Summaries are contained in F. S. Regs., Part II. and the Staff Manual respectively. Title pages will be prepared in manuscript.

Place	Date	Hour	Summary of Events and Information	Remarks and references to Appendices
G.17.B.6.0.				
In the field	1.	1.30	Fired 10 rounds	
	2	5 P.M.	" 11 "	
	3	9 A.M.	" 13 "	
	5	11 P.M.	" 40 "	
	6	6.30 P.M.	" 4 "	
	7	11 A.M.	" 45 "	
	8	all night	" 29 "	
	10	5.45 A.M.	" 21 "	
	11 to 13	9 A.M.	Battery on the march.	
	13 -		End of march. Standing by but not in action.	

Total for month 173

S.H. Skewes 2nd Lt. & San. Lt. ?
O.C. Y/21 T.M. Battery

Army Form C. 2118.

WAR DIARY
or
INTELLIGENCE SUMMARY.
(Erase heading not required.)

Y/21 Trench Mortar Batty

Place	Date	Hour	Summary of Events and Information	Remarks and references to Appendices
A27 D28	Oct 1. to 15th		Battery out in action. Provided working parties for R.F.A.	
	15-			
	21st		Batty on the march	
	22nd		Took on the line	
	23		" " "	
	24th		Fired 21 rounds. Total for the day Fired 63 rounds	
	25th		" 21 "	
	26		" 21 "	One Enfield mount was hit - lost 20 cartridges - except loss of 18 rounds sustained.	
	27th			

E H Skinner 2nd Lieut
O.C. Y/21 T.M.B.

WAR DIARY
or
~~INTELLIGENCE~~ SUMMARY

Y.ii Trench Mortar Bn.y Nov. 1916.

Army Form C. 2118.

Place	Date	Hour	Summary of Events and Information	Remarks and references to Appendices
Mh.36.c NW.I. M.64. a.9.6	Oct 29 - 31st	Fired	172 rounds.	
	Nov 1 - 10th	Fired	342 "	
	11th - 20th	Fired	254 "	
	21 - 27	Fired	169 "	

nothing to report 6 rounds for the month

S H Skaim Lt
8th Son TM
O C Y.i T.M.B.

Army Form C. 2118.

Y/21 Medium Trench
Mortar Battery
December 16.

WAR DIARY
or
INTELLIGENCE SUMMARY.
(Erase heading not required.)

Place	Date	Hour	Summary of Events and Information	Remarks and references to Appendices
Map 36cNW3 24c	Nov 28 to 30.		Fired 63 Rounds	
	Dec 1 to 10.		" 253 "	
	" 11 to 20.		" 289 "	
	" 21 to 29.		" 197 "	

Yeats
Capt R.G.A.
Command^g T.M.B.

21st Divisional Artillery.

Late 51st Trench Mortar Battery

Z/21 TRENCH MORTAR BATTERY

MARCH TO DECEMBER 1916.

6-7-16

From O.C.
    Trench Mortar Bde

To D.A.G.
    3rd Echelon.
        Base.

Herewith War Diaries for the month of June 1916 rendered by the following Batteries under my command.

V. W. X. Y. Z.   21st Trench Mortar Batteries

E J Davis Capt. GS.
Commanding 21st T M BDE.

Army Form C. 2118.

WAR DIARY
or
INTELLIGENCE SUMMARY
Z 21 French Mortar Battery
Lieut Col. 5th Z.M.Bty

(Erase heading not required).

Instructions regarding War Diaries and Intelligence Summaries are contained in F. S. Regs., Part II, and the Staff Manual respectively. Title Pages will be prepared in manuscript.

Place	Date	Hour	Summary of Events and Information	Remarks and references to Appendices
5th Corps Area	March 1st		Building emplacements and bringing up ammunition for two 2" guns at St. Eloi.	
	2nd		Stood by all day and all night during action at the Bluff. That did not actually go into action.	
	3rd		Stood by all day. Snow caused the emplacements to be partly flooded and work was resumed to rebuild them.	
	4th		Rebuilding emplacements	
	5th		— do —	
	6th		— do —	
	7th		— do —	
	8th		Emplacements rebuilt and handed over to 17th Division. Trench Mortars together with ammunition	
	9th		Battery returned to Armentieres.	

W.F. Robertson 2nd Lt
for O.C. Z 21 Trench Mortar Bty.

Army Form C. 2118.

WAR DIARY
or
INTELLIGENCE SUMMARY

Z 21 Trench Mortar Battery

(Erase heading not required).

Instructions regarding War Diaries and Intelligence Summaries are contained in F. S. Regs., Part II, and the Staff Manual respectively. Title Pages will be prepared in manuscript.

Sheet N⁰ 36 N.W.

Place	Date	Hour	Summary of Events and Information	Remarks and references to Appendices
	March 10th		Battery resting after returning from 5th Corps area.	
C.23.D.3.0.	11th			
	12th		Took over one 2" gun and one 1½" gun from 45th Trench Mortar Battery in centre sector.	
	13th		Building new dugout and emplacement in Yser Avenue.	
	14th		— ditto —. Cleaned out bomb-store	
	15th		— ditto —.	
	16th		— ditto —	

W. Y. Robertson 2 Lt
for O.C. Trench Mortar Battery

Army Form C. 2118.

WAR DIARY
or
INTELLIGENCE SUMMARY   Z 2 / Trench Mortar Battery
(Erase heading not required).

Instructions regarding War Diaries and Intelligence
Summaries are contained in F. S. Regs., Part II,
and the Staff Manual respectively. Title Pages
will be prepared in manuscript.

Sheet No 36 N.W.

Place	Date	Hour	Summary of Events and Information	Remarks and references to Appendices
C 28 d 3.0.	March 17th		Preparing emplacement for 1½" gun in Trench 79.	
	18th	5 p.m.	Fired 25 light 1½" bombs from emplacement in 79 trench, at the wire and front trenches of the Port Ballot salient (C29 a 3½, 1½). All the bombs detonated well and considerable damage was caused to the German knife rests and wire entanglements.	
	19th		Clearing up emplacements and trench stores.	
	20th		— ditto —	
	21st		Handed over positions, guns and stores to 17th Division Trench Mortars.	
	22nd		— ditto —	
	23rd		Left Armentières for rest billets	

W.G. Robertson H
for O.C. Trench Mortar Battery

Army Form C. 2118.

WAR DIARY
or
INTELLIGENCE SUMMARY   221 Trench Mortar Battery
(Erase heading not required).

Instructions regarding War Diaries and Intelligence Summaries are contained in F. S. Regs., Part II, and the Staff Manual respectively. Title Pages will be prepared in manuscript.

Place	Date	Hour	Summary of Events and Information	Remarks and references to Appendices
Booze	March 23rd		Resting: Ordinary Training	
	24th			
	25th			
	26th			
	27th			
	28th			
	29th			
	30th			
	31st			

W. J. Robertson 2/Lt
for O.C. Trench Mortar Battery

Army Form C. 2118.

WAR DIARY
or
INTELLIGENCE SUMMARY

(Erase heading not required).

2" Trench Mortar Battery 2" gun
April 30th 1916

Instructions regarding War Diaries and Intelligence Summaries are contained in F. S. Regs., Part II, and the Staff Manual respectively. Title Pages will be prepared in manuscript.

Place	Date	Hour	Summary of Events and Information	Remarks and references to Appendices
Park 62 D NE 2	1-16		Battery in rear billets. Building emplacements.	
	17			
	18		Find of all arrangements of parts on enemies Trench Mortar	
	19		Work on emplacement	
	20			
	21		Find 12 as above	
	22			
F2 B35	23		This Battery having taken over a new line that had previously	
	24		2" Trench Mortar emplacements all time was spent building new	
	25			
	26			
	27			
	28			
	29			
	30			

Graham H/Capt
T.M.B.
2" T.M. —

Army Form C. 2118.

1. **WAR DIARY** or **INTELLIGENCE SUMMARY**
Z 21. Trench Mortar Bty.
(Erase heading not required).

Place	Date	Hour	Summary of Events and Information	Remarks and references to Appendices
Map 62D N.E.2 F26.1½.4½	May 1	6pm	Fired 5 rounds retaliation to Stokes Trench Mortar from Z.26.6.18. Shooting very effective – Enemy machine gun silenced Map 57 D S.E.4	
			Fired 5 rounds retaliation to rifle grenades from F.26.5.25. Target F3a.6½.4½	
		7.15pm	Fired 4 rounds retaliation to rifle Grenades from F26.5.25. Target F3a.5.3	
		8 pm	Fired 5 rounds retaliation to Enemy Trench + rifle Grenades from F26.5.25. Silenced enemy Trench Mortar	
	May 2	1.15pm	Fired 2 rounds retaliation to rifle Grenades from F.26.5.25	
		3 pm	1 " " " enemy sniper at Z.27.c.2.4 from Z.26.d.30	
		7.30pm	5 " " from F.26.5.25 } Retaliation for Trench Mortars	
			9 " " " F3.c.12 } + rifle grenades	
	May 3	6 am to 2 pm	3 " " " F.26.5.25	— do —
		2.30 pm	6 " " " "	Target Bosch Sap from F3a.53 to F3a.65.30. Some direct hits obtained + much timber + trench material was blown up. 9 Kanti Dr.RFA

Army Form C. 2118.

WAR DIARY
or
INTELLIGENCE SUMMARY

Z.21 Trench Mortar Bty

No. 2.

(Erase heading not required).

Instructions regarding War Diaries and Intelligence Summaries are contained in F. S. Regs., Part II, and the Staff Manual respectively. Title Pages will be prepared in manuscript.

Place	Date	Hour	Summary of Events and Information	Remarks and references to Appendices
Map 62 c NE 2	May 3 cont.	8 pm	Fired 3 rounds from F3c12 } Retaliation to Trench Mortar	
			" 3 " " X26a30 } + rifle grenades	
F2 61½ w/h	May 4	4 am	" 3 " " F26b5.25 — do —	
		3 pm	" 3 " " X26a30 — do —	
		3 pm to 5 pm	" 8 " " F26b5.25 — do —	
			" 4 " " F26b5.25 } — do —	
		8.30 pm	" 12 " " F3c12 — do —	
	May 5	4.45 pm	" 6 " " F26b5.25 — do —	
		5.15 pm	" 2 " " X26a30 — do —	
		10.30 pm	" 2 " " F26b5.25 — do —	
		11 pm	" 4 " " F3c12 — do —	
	6/12		13 Battery making	

R. White Lt. R.F.A.

BSD - B. M351/22/11. 12/15. 2000

Army Form C. 2118.

WAR DIARY
or
INTELLIGENCE SUMMARY $\underline{Z\ 21\ Trench\ Mortar\ B\underline{t}y}$

(Erase heading not required.)

Instructions regarding War Diaries and Intelligence Summaries are contained in F.S. Regs., Part II, and the Staff Manual respectively. Title Pages will be prepared in manuscript.

Place	Date	Hour	Summary of Events and Information	Remarks and references to Appendices
Map 62D. NE 2 F27.d.4.4½	May 13	2.22 am	Fired 1 round from Z.26.d.30 to cover explosion by raiding parts at Z.26.d.3.3½. Blowing up bank wire.	
			In connection with the same scheme we fired 5 rounds at 1½ min intervals from F.9.a.3½.8 at target F.3.c.7.5½	
	May 14th	11 am	Fired 3 rounds from F.27.b.65.25. Retaliation to trench mortar rifle grenades	
		6 pm	" 6 " " Z.26.d.30 do	
	May 15 5 am to 7 am	21	" F.26.b.65.25 at target F.3.a.44 with the object of harassing enemy trench + wires; intermittent work – destroying trench + emplacements which was known to exist at this point. We obtained 17 direct hits on his trench + wire + parapet at this trench was knocked in several places. The machine gun did not fire again from this point for some time.	
		6 am	Fired 2 rounds retaliation to rifle grenades from F.26.b.5.25	
		3.57 pm	" 16 " from F.3.c.0.4½ at target enemy trench F.3.c.9.1	

Much damage was done to enemy trench + wire.   F.L.Abbott Lt. R.F.a

Army Form C. 2118.

WAR DIARY
or
INTELLIGENCE SUMMARY

No. 4. Z.21 Trench Mortar Bty.

(Erase heading not required).

Place	Date	Hour	Summary of Events and Information	Remarks and references to Appendices
Map 62 D N.E.2. F.2.b.1½.4½	May 15th (Contd)	4.15 a.m	Fired 17 rounds from F.2.b.65.25. } Retaliation for Boshe Trench Mortars & Rifle grenades	
			" 6 " " X.26.d.3.0. }	
	16th	5 a.m	Fired 5 " " " " —do—	
			" 7 " " F.3.c.0.4½	
			" 10 " " F.2.b.65.25. In all this retaliation we succeeded in having the last word and fired about twice as many rounds as the enemy.	
		3 h.m.	Fired 11 rounds from F.9.a.3½.8. at Target F.3.c.7.5½	
		6 "	" 10 " " F.3.c.0.4½ " " F.3.c.9.1.	
		5 h.m.	The shooting was good and several direct hits were obtained on the enemy's Trench & considerable quantities of material blown up.	
		4 h.m.	Fired 2 rounds from X.26.d.3.0. retaliation for Rifle grenade	
			" 1 " " F.2.b.65.25 } retaliation for Trench Mortars & rifle grenades	
		8.15 p.m	" 6 " " X.26.d.3.0	
			" 2 " " F.3.c.0.4½	

W.G. Robertson 2nd Connaught Rangers
for O.C. Z.21. T.M. Bty.

Army Form C. 2118.

WAR DIARY
or
INTELLIGENCE SUMMARY   Z.21 Trench Mortar Bty

(Erase heading not required).

Place	Date	Hour	Summary of Events and Information	Remarks and references to Appendices
Map D 62 N.E.2. F.2.b. 1/2.4 1/2	May 17th	4h.m	Fired 4 rounds from F.2.b.65.25. Retaliation for Rifle grenades.	
	17"	9h.m	" 7 " " " " "	
	18th	4h.m to 8h.m	" 19 " " " " Trench Mortars	
		4.30 p.m	" 6 " " X.26.d.3.0. " "	
	19th 20 24		Battery Resting.	
	25th	2 a.m	Fired 3 rounds from F.2.b.65.25 } Retaliation for Rifle grenades Target F.3.a.60.67.	
		2.15 a.m	" 2 " " " - do -	
		9.30 p.m	" 6 " " } Retaliation for Trench Mortars	
			" 5 " " X 26.d. 3.0	
		11h.m	" 10 " " F.3.c.o. 4 1/2 - do -	

W.G. Robertson 2 Lieut
3rd Connaught Rangers
for O.C. Z.2, T. M. Bty.

Army Form C. 2118.

WAR DIARY
or
INTELLIGENCE SUMMARY Z.21. French Mortar Bty.
(Erase heading not required).

Instructions regarding War Diaries and Intelligence Summaries are contained in F. S. Regs., Part II, and the Staff Manual respectively. Title Pages will be prepared in manuscript.

Place	Date	Hour	Summary of Events and Information	Remarks and references to Appendices
Map 62 D N.E.2.	May 26th	1.30 p.m.	Fired 6 rounds from F.3.c.0.4½. Target F.3.c.9.1. retaliation for French Mortars.	
F.2.b.1½.4½		2.30 p.m.	Fired 1 round from " " " " " for Trench Mortars	
		7 p.m.	Fired 5 rounds from " " " " " for Trench Mortars	
		7.30 p.m.	Fired 1 round from " " " " " for Trench Mortars	
		8.30 p.m.	Fired 3 rounds from " " " " " for French Mortars	" } retaliation for French Mortars & rifle grenades
	27th	3 A.M.	Fired 6 rounds from F.2.b.6.5.25. " F.3.a.8057	
			" 5 " " X.26.d.3.0.	
			" 6 " " X.26.d.3.0. " X.27.c.2.4 } retaliation for Trench Mortars
		2.45 p.m.	" 10 " " F.2.b.65.35. " F.3.a.6067
			" 2 " " " F.3.c.7.5½ — do —
		4 p.m.	" 6 " " F.9.a.3½.9. " " "

W.G. Robertson 2/Lieut 3rd Connaught Rangers
for O.C. Z.21. T.M.Bty.

Army Form C. 2118.

WAR DIARY
or
INTELLIGENCE SUMMARY Z.21. Trench Mortar Bty.
(Erase heading not required)

Instructions regarding War Diaries and Intelligence Summaries are contained in F. S. Regs., Part II, and the Staff Manual respectively. Title Pages will be prepared in manuscript.

Place	Date	Hour	Summary of Events and Information	Remarks and references to Appendices
MAP 62 N.E.2. F.2.&1½.4½	May 28th	3.a.m	Fired 18 rounds from F.2.6.65.25 } retaliation for a heavy " 12 " X.26.d.3.0 } bombardment of Trench " 1 " F.9.a. 3½.8 } Mortars & howitzers. The shooting was very effective and succeeded in silencing the hostile French Mortars.	
		3.p.m	Fired 6 rounds from X.26.d.3.0. The shooting was very good and the German front trench was considerably damaged.	
		4.15 p.m	Fired 17 rounds from X.36.d.3.0. Target X.26.d.9½.5.& X.27.c.3.4. Fired 12 rounds from F.2.6.65.25. Target F.3.a.6067. in retaliation for Trench Mortars, after a few rounds the enemy trench mortars ceased fire.	
		8.45 p.m	Fired 12 rounds from F.2.6.65.25. Target F.3.a.6067 } in retaliation to French Mortars Fired 4 rounds from X.26.d.3.0. retaliation to Trench Mortars	
	May 29th	14.m	Fired 1 ranging shot from F.2.6.65.25. Battery went out to rest	

W.G. Robertson Lieut
for O.C. Z. 21. T.M. Bty.
Connaught Rangers

Army Form C. 2118.

WAR DIARY
or
INTELLIGENCE SUMMARY

Z 21 Trench Mortar By
July 1916

(Erase heading not required.)

Instructions regarding War Diaries and Intelligence Summaries are contained in F. S. Regs., Part II. and the Staff Manual respectively. Title Pages will be prepared in manuscript.

Place	Date	Hour	Summary of Events and Information	Remarks and references to Appendices
Maps 57 SE 4 Q26 B 28	June 1 6 June 5		The battery supplied working parties to build emplacements.	
	5/12		The battery was mostly not of the trenches	
	13		Fired 44 rounds in retaliation to Rifle grenades + Sausages	
	14		" 73 " "	
	15		Worked on emplacement + trenches	
	16		Fired 34 rounds in retaliation to Sausages	
	17/23		Working on Emplacements + trenches	
	24		Fired 305 rounds — Cutting wire at Bock first line + Back	
	25		" 208 " " " day, battery a few shots on Spanlly	
	26		" 74 " " "	
	27		" 150 " " " Route into trenches from emplacement.	
	28		" 104 " " " Sunken road is in three parts of front +	
	29		" 74 " " " support lines where were written in	
	30		" 110 " " "	
	July 1		" 70 rounds on Bock first line in conjunction with Artillery & from heavy bombardment preparatory to infantry attack	

J. A. [?] Capt
OC Z 21 T M B.

Army Form C. 2118.

WAR DIARY
or
INTELLIGENCE SUMMARY Z 21 Trench Mortar By
(Erase heading not required.) July 1st/16.

Place	Date	Hour	Summary of Events and Information	Remarks and references to Appendices
Map 57 SE 4 R 26 b 28			Remarks on the Shooting of 1095 rounds by Z 2, T.M.B5. in the preliminary bombardment June 24 to July 1st 1916. The NEWTON D.A. fuze used on this occasion for wire cutting proved excellent in every way, & the work allotted to the battery was easily & satisfactorily performed. The ammunition was very good & only 1% were blinds. On the whole the strain on the lever fuzes caused a large number of casualties to equipment, especially to rifle mechanisms, which had to be replaced two fifty times. One fuze (No 13) was completely blown out by a direct hit, which also detonated about 30 rounds of ammunition. The reports of this Shooting form that 2" Trench Mortars are most satisfactory when used for wire cutting with the NEWTON, D.A. fuze, although the strain on the present establishment of personnel is heavy. The T.M.B5. casualties to the battery were :- Wounded. 1 Offr. O.R. J.F.Mchr. Capt 2 OC Z 2, T.M.B5.	

WAR DIARY or INTELLIGENCE SUMMARY

Army Form C. 2118

July 1916 Z/21 Medium Trench Mortar Battery

Vol 1

Place	Date 1916	Hour	Summary of Events and Information	Remarks and references to Appendices
Map 62D N E 2	July 1st 5 15		Battery in rest at Billets at E. 17. C.	
	16th		Battery ascisted to get 2" trench Mortar Guns and Ammunition in action in Mametz Wood.	
	17th 18 19 20th		Battery resting in Billets.	
	21st		Battery lent to 33rd Division proceeded with guns and ammunition to Bazentin Wood, but services were not required.	
	22nd		Resting in Billets.	
	24th 25		Battery made two journeys to bring guns and ammunition back.	
	26th 27 28 29		On line of March	
	31.		Resting in Billets	

J.D.D. Allen
Lieut Dorsets
For O.C. Z.21. Medium Trench Mortar By

Army Form C. 2118.

Z/21 Trench Mortar Battery Vol 8

WAR DIARY
or
INTELLIGENCE SUMMARY.
(Erase heading not required.)

Instructions regarding War Diaries and Intelligence Summaries are contained in F.S. Regs., Part II. and the Staff Manual respectively. Title pages will be prepared in manuscript.

Place	Date	Hour	Summary of Events and Information	Remarks and references to Appendices
MAP 51 B. N.W.1. A.29.F.	August 1st–2nd	—	Battery in Rest billets	
	3rd	—	Took over two 2-inch guns and one 1½" gun from 14th Division	
	4th	4:20 p.m.	Fired 10 rounds from 2" gun (A.30.c.2.7.) Target: A.30.c.55.65	
		2.6 p.m.	" " " " " " (A.30.c.2.7.) Target: A.30.c.55.95	
			" " " " " " (A.29.d.7.0.) Target: A.30.c.55.95	
			This was in retaliation to German Trench Mortars which ceased firing after we had sent over about 6 rounds.	
	5th–6th	—	Replenished bombstores at gun positions	
	7th	1:30 p.m.	Fired 78 rounds from 2" gun (A.29.d.7.0.) & 5 rounds 2" gun (A.30.c.2.7.) Retaliation for a German Trench Mortar.	
		4.1 p.m.	Fired 6 rounds from 2" gun (A.30.c.2.7.) Retaliation to hostile Trench Mortars.	
	8th	—	Replenished bombstores.	
	9th	3 a.m.	Fired 5 rounds 2" from (A.29.d.7.0.) & 2 rounds 2" from (A.30.c.2.7.) in retaliation to 2 German Trench Mortars	
	10th	—	Replenished bombstores.	
	11th	4:30 p.m. 6 p.m.	Fired 10 rounds 2" (A.30.c.2.7.) & 6 rounds 2" (A.29.d.7.0.) Retaliation to Trench Mortars.	
	12th	8 a.m.	Fired 20 rounds 2" (" " ") x 13 (" " ") x 6 8 " "	
	13th	3:30 p.m.	" " " (" " ") x 4 " " " "	

W.G. Robertson, 2 Lieut
O.C. Z/21 Trench Mortar Battery

Army Form C. 2118

WAR DIARY or INTELLIGENCE SUMMARY

Z.21. Trench Mortar Battery

(Erase heading not required.)

Place	Date August	Hour	Summary of Events and Information	Remarks and references to Appendices
Map 51 B. N.W. 1. A. 29. b.	14	9 a.m.	Fired 27 rounds 2" on German front trenches (A.30.c.55.65 to A.30.c.50.50) from 2" gun (A.30.c.2.7). Shooting very good. Much material (duckboards & revetment).	
		6 p.m.	Was blown up. Fired 15 rounds 2" from (A.30.c.55.2.7) & 10 rounds 2" from (A.29.d.7.0) Retaliation to German "sausages".	
	15	3 p.m.	Fired 11 rounds 2" from (A.30.c.2.7) + 15 rounds 2" from (A.29.d.7.0) Retaliation to hostile T.M.s	
	16	4 p.m.	" 30 " " " "	
	17	6 p.m.	" 15 " " " "	
	18	2.30 p.m.	" 8 " " " "	
	19	3 p.m.	" 25 " " " "	
	20	6.30 p.m.	" 24 " " " "	
	21	1.15 p.m.	" 5 " " " "	
	22	6 p.m.	" 10 " " " "	
			In all these shoots our Trench Mortars got the upper hand and succeeded in firing an average of 6 rounds to every German round sent over.	
	23	1.30 p.m.	Fired 13 rounds 3" from (A.30.c.27) Retaliation for 3 rifle grenades (A.29.d.7.0) " " French Mortars	
		6 p.m.	" 16 " " " "	
	24	6 p.m.	Fired 25 1/2" bombs (slight 17 Liens). The shooting was splendid. Every one except 3 hit the target (listening post A.30.c.50.90). The 3 that did not hit, the target fell on the enemy wire and dislodged two large panels with there were 2 planks. There was no retaliation whatever.	
	25	4 p.m.	Fired 6, 2" bombs from (A.30.b.9.7) + 1, 1/2" bomb. Retaliation to hostile T.M.s	2
		5 p.m.	" 11 " " (A.29.d.7.0)	5
		12 noon	" 6 " " (A.30.c.9.17)	2 small
	26	2 p.m.	" 10 " " " Ranging shots with Newton at.	

Total fired from August 1st to 26th 3" 443 } 469
2" 26

W.J. Robertson 2nd Lieut.
O.C. Z.21. Trench Mortar Battery

Army Form C. 2118.

WAR DIARY
or
INTELLIGENCE SUMMARY.
(Erase heading not required.)

Z.1 Trench Mortar Battery

Instructions regarding War Diaries and Intelligence Summaries are contained in F. S. Regs., Part II. and the Staff Manual respectively. Title pages will be prepared in manuscript.

Place	Date	Hour	Summary of Events and Information	Remarks and references to Appendices
MAP 51B NW.1 Rodincourt A.29.6.	August			
	27th	2.30 p.m.	Fired 14 rounds (2") and 8 rounds (1½") from A.30.C.2.7. in retaliation to German Trench Mortar Bombs	
		11.30 p.m.	Fired 7 rounds (2") from A.29.d.7.0. in retaliation to 1 German Trench Mortar Bomb	
	28th	8.1. p.m.	Fired 8 rounds (2") from A.29.d.7.0 in retaliation to 2 Trench Mortar Bombs	
	29th	6.30 p.m.	" 7 " (2") " A.30.C.2.7. " 1 " "	
	30th	4.0 p.m.	" 22 " (2") " A.30.C.2.7. & A.29.d.7.0 " 6 " "	
	31st	2.30 p.m.	" 32 " (2") " " " " "	
	Sept.			
	1st	3 p.m.	" 11 " (2") " from A.30.C.2.7. in retaliation to German Trench Mortars	
	2nd	8.30 p.m.	" 3 " (2") " from A.30.C.2.7. " " " " 1 " Bomb	
	3rd		Emplacements at A.30.C.2.7. & A.29.d.7.0. deepened by 3 feet and overhead cover placed above.	
	4th		Work on above emplacements. No trouble from German 'minnenwerfers'	
	5th	8.30 p.m.	Fired 12 rounds (2") from A.30.C.2.7. retaliation to 2 " "	
			" 9 " (2") " A.29.d.7.0 " " "	
	6th	6.50 p.m.	" 56 " (2") " + A.30.C.2.7. " 9 " "	
			The shooting was very good and effectively silenced the "Bombs"	

W.J. Robertson 2 Lieut
O.C. Z.21. Trench Mortar Bty

Army Form C. 2118.

WAR DIARY
or
INTELLIGENCE SUMMARY.
(Erase heading not required.)

Z.21. Trench Mortar Battery

②

Instructions regarding War Diaries and Intelligence Summaries are contained in F.S. Regs., Part II. and the Staff Manual respectively. Title pages will be prepared in manuscript.

Place	Date	Hour	Summary of Events and Information	Remarks and references to Appendices
Map 51^B N.W.1. Rodincourt. A.29.b.	Sept 7th		Fired 14 rounds (2") retaliation to 3 German 'minenwerfers'	
	8th		" 76 rounds (2") " " 8 " "	
			The shooting was very effective and silenced the German machines.	
	9th		Fired 85 rounds (2") retaliation to German minenwerfer	
	10th		Handed over to 35th Division	
		9.30 a.m.	left Arras proceeded to Warnin	
	10th to 13th		Resting at Warnin	
	13th to 16th		Left Warnin arrived Albert 14th	
	14th to 27th		Battery acting as working party on roads and/or carrying ammunition etc on Mametz and Longueval.	
			Total fired from August 27th to Sept 27th 2" 355 ⎱ 363 12" 8 ⎰

W.J. Robertson, 2/Lieut
O.C. Z.21 Trench Mortar Battery

WAR DIARY or **INTELLIGENCE SUMMARY.**
(Erase heading not required.)

Z 21 Trench Mortar Battery

Army Form C. 2118.

Place	Date	Hour	Summary of Events and Information	Remarks and references to Appendices
A27 D28	Oct 1st to 13th		Battery provided working parties for R.F.A. on the Somme	
	15th		Marched from Somme to Bethune.	
	16 "			
	21 "			
	22 "		Took over from 8th Division	
	23 "		Cleaned guns & replenished trenchstore.	
	24 "	3pm	Fired 7 rounds from G.18.b.2.7 } retaliation to three	
			" 8 " " G.18.45.90 } German T.M.'s	
	25 "	6.30 "	" 5 " " G.18.b.27 } — ditto — two	
			" 3 " " G.18.45.90 }	
	26 "	3pm to 4 "	" 25 " " G.18.b.27 } Wire cutting. Result very	
			" 20 " " G.18.45.90 } satisfactory	
	27 "	"	" 41 " " G.18.b.45.90 Retaliation to German Microwurfer	

W.G. Robertson Lieut
O.C. Z.21 French Mortar Batty

WAR DIARY
~~INTELLIGENCE SUMMARY~~

Army Form C. 2118.

Z.21. French Mortar Battery

Place	Date	Hour	Summary of Events and Information	Remarks and references to Appendices
Map. N.W.36.c.	**Mar.** 1st		Fired 21 rounds 2" cutting wire at (H.7.c.00.55 to H.7.c.00.35.)	
			" 13 rounds in retaliation to a few Boshe Trench Mortar Bombs.	
	2nd		" 27 rounds 2" cutting wire at (H.7.c.00.55 to H.7.c.00.35.) + (G.12.d.3.9 & G.12.d.5.8)	
	3rd		" 20 rounds on Boshe front line at (G.12.d.9.2 & G.12.d.5.2) Considerable damage was caused but the enemy did not retaliate.	
	4th		Fired 24 rounds in retaliation to four German T.M. bombs	
	5th		" 40 rounds on support lines at (G.12.a.4.0 & G.12.a.9.1) in conjunction with Stokes guns. Although much trouble and wire was disturbed the enemy did not retaliate.	
	6th		Fired 36 rounds in conjunction with Stokes guns on G.12.a.4.0	
	7th		Fired 19 rounds in retaliation to five Boshe T.M.'s (& G.12.a.9.1.)	
			Total fired for week 200	

W.J. Robertson Lieut
O.C. Z.21. T.M.By.

WAR DIARY or INTELLIGENCE SUMMARY

Army Form C. 2118.

Z 21 Trench Mortar Battery (2)

Place	Date	Hour	Summary of Events and Information	Remarks and references to Appendices
N.W. 36.c.	Nov 8th		Fired 13 rounds on G.12.d.30.95 to G.12.d.45.80 retaliation to T.M.s	
	9th		" 34 rounds on (G.12.a.9.0. & G.17.a.9.1.) in conjunction with Stokes guns. Considerable damage was done but no retaliation.	
	10th		Fired 39 rounds in retaliation to four Boche T.M.s	
	11th		" 40 " " " " about ten "Boche" T.M.s	
	12th		" 37 " " " " Six Boche T.M.s	
	13th		" 35 " " " " about four Boche T.M.s	
	14th		" 33 " offensive shooting on Boche front and support lines from H.13.a.2.9. to G.13.a.9.1.	
	15th		Fired 36 rounds in retaliation to a few T.M.s	
	16th		" 84 rounds on Boche front and support lines from H.13.a.2.9. to G.13.a.9.1. retaliation for his activity during the last five days. Considerable damage was done and enemy did not retaliate.	
	17th		Fired 54 rounds at same target as on the 16th.	
			Total for 10 days : 405	

W.J. Robertson Lieut
O.C. Z 21 T.M.B.y.

Army Form C. 2118.

WAR DIARY
or
INTELLIGENCE SUMMARY. Z 21 T.M. Bɣ.
(Erase heading not required.)

(3)

Instructions regarding War Diaries and Intelligence Summaries are contained in F.S. Regs., Part II. and the Staff Manual respectively. Title pages will be prepared in manuscript.

Place	Date	Hour	Summary of Events and Information	Remarks and references to Appendices
Maps N.M.36C.	Nov 18th		Fired 25 rounds on Boche front line at G12 a 4.9. & G12 a 9.1.	
	19th		" 29 rounds on " " " G12 d 30v5 & G12 d 30	
	20th		" 72 " retaliation to about 20 enemy T.M.s	
	21st		" 34 " to four enemy T.M.s	
	22		" 20 " during a small bombardment preliminary to an enemy raid on our trenches.	
			" 32 rounds from 2.30 a.m. to 2.95 a.m. in conjunction with Stokes guns & artillery. Shooting was very effective endangering deal of damage was done at (G12 a 9.9. & G12 a 9.1)	
	23rd		Nothing to report.	
	24th		Fired 34 rounds retaliation to a few Boche T.M.s	
	25th		Fired 43 rounds on (B12 c c 9 & G12 c 7.9) A machine gun Officers to have been destroyed during this shot.	
	26th		No report. The enemy has not been nearly so active from Nov 1st to Nov 26th as he was during October, with the exception of Nov 20th to Nov 22nd. Total for 9 days: 289 W.J. Robertson Lieut.
			Total for 26 days: 894 O.C. Z 21 T.M. Bɣ.	

Army Form C. 2118.

WAR DIARY
or
INTELLIGENCE SUMMARY.
(Erase heading not required.)

Z 21 Trench Mortar Battery

December /16

Place	Date	Hour	Summary of Events and Information	Remarks and references to Appendices
N.W. LOOS 36CW.W.3 G.11.d	1916 December 1st		Fired nil as all guns were out of action owing to broken rifle mechanisms	
	2nd		Fired 20 rounds at German trench line at H7.C.0.3 to H7.C.1.2	
	3rd		Fired 20 rounds Ditto (Much timber was blown up.)	
	4th		Fired 25 " on H7.C.1106 to H7.C.1.2.	
	5th		In conjunction with the Artillery two guns were in action from 12 noon to 2 p.m. Target was enemy wire in front of Bodies Trenches H7.C.1106 to H7.C.03. Wire was greatly damaged. 35 rounds were fired. All guns out of action.	
	6th		Fired 30 rounds on German wire from H7.C.0.0.4 to H7.C.1101.	
	7th		Fired 40 rounds at following targets (i) (Wire from H7.C.1109 to H7.C.0053) with very good results.	
	8th		(ii) Wire H7.C.1106 to H7.C.03)	
	9th		Fired 65 rounds at enemy wire (from H7.C.1109 to H7.C.0053) The wire was greatly damaged and several gaps were made	
			Rounds fired from Dec 1st to 9th : 235	

W. J. Robertson Lieut
O.C. Z 21 Trench Mortar Battery

Army Form C. 2118.

WAR DIARY or INTELLIGENCE SUMMARY.

(Erase heading not required.)

Z.21 Trench Mortar Battery

Instructions regarding War Diaries and Intelligence Summaries are contained in F. S. Regs., Part II. and the Staff Manual respectively. Title pages will be prepared in manuscript.

Place	Date	Hour	Summary of Events and Information	Remarks and references to Appendices
Loos 36 C N.W.3 G.11.d	1916 December 10th		Fired 65 rounds on German wire (from H.7.c.11.0.9.5 – H.7.c.00.5.3)	
	11th		Fired 17 rounds after which all guns were out of action through broken rifle mechanisms.	
	12th		Fired 39 rounds at German front line at B.12.d.50.65 with very good results.	
	13th		Fired 25 rounds retaliation to German T.M. fire.	
	14th		Fired 50 rounds on German front line and wire with excellent results. A large gap was made at G.12.d.91.61 and a smaller one at H.7.c.0.4.	
	15th		Fired 45 rounds on following targets (i) H.7.c.0.9. (got in more entrances) (ii) G.12.d.91.61 (got in wire enlarged) (iii) G.12.c.57 & G.12.a.21. (Front Trench)	
	16th		Fired 25 rounds retaliation to German T.M.s	
	17th		Fired 34 rounds on following targets (i) Wire from H.7.c.0.4 to G.12.d.9.6 (ii) Wire G.12.c.5.9 & G.12.a.9.1.	
	18th		Fired 44 rounds on enemy front & support lines around G.12.a.5.1.	
	19th		Fired 39 rounds at H.7.c.0.6 & H.7.c.12 & enemy supports around G.12.a.5.1.	
			Total fired from Dec 10th to Dec 19th 378 Rounds	

W.J. Robertson Lieut.
O.C. Z.21 Trench Mortar Battery

Army Form C. 2118.

WAR DIARY
or
INTELLIGENCE SUMMARY.
(Erase heading not required.)

Z.21 Trench Mortar Battery

Place	Date	Hour	Summary of Events and Information	Remarks and references to Appendices
Nr. LOOS. 36 C N W 3 G.11.d	1915 December 20th		Fired 23 rounds on enemy Trenches around G.12.a.4.1 with excellent results.	
	21st		Two guns at G.13.t.45.80 & G.13.t.45.93 took part in a combined shoot with the Artillery lasting from 1.30 to 2.30 p.m. The Targets were H.7.c.0.4 & H.7.c.1.5.42. & H.7.c.0.5.60 & G.12.a.9.7. 73 rounds were fired and the damage done was very great the parapet being breached in several places & much Trench being destroyed	
	22nd		Fired 50 rounds in retaliation to about the German T.M. rounds	
	23rd		Germans started a heavy bombardment with T.M.'s & Artillery we fired 30 rounds in retaliation and then kept the rest in reserve in case of an attack	
	24th		Germans still kept up the bombardment and we retaliated with 46 rounds.	
	25th		Not fired, as Infantry were digging some new out of a sap.	
	26th		Fired 37 rounds retaliation to German T.M.'s Total fired 20th to 26th December : 259 rounds Total fired from Dec 1st to Dec 26th : 872 rounds	

W.J. Robertson Lieut
O.C. Z.21 French Mortar Battery

WAR DIARY
or
INTELLIGENCE SUMMARY.
(Erase heading not required.)

Army Form C. 2118.

Place	Date	Hour	Summary of Events and Information	Remarks and references to Appendices
	January 1917		231 Trench Mortar Battery	
			The Battery moved out of the Line on the 4th – 14th January and proceeded to Rest Billets. Parades were held daily for Physical Drill and Rifle Drill. The Battery moved from Rest Billets at the end of the month.	
	24th January 1917			

J. Phipps Major
Comdg. 231 T.M. Battery

Army Form C. 2118.

WAR DIARY
or
INTELLIGENCE SUMMARY.
(Erase heading not required.)

1/21 T.M. Btty.

Place	Date	Hour	Summary of Events and Information	Remarks and references to Appendices
	1/1/17 – 4/1/17		1/21 T.M. battery had four guns in action just north of the ground opposite Wied St Elie. Hostile T.M's were very troublesome, firing at the line & at our guns. R.F.C. up a fair average, in retaliation.	
	4/1/17		Relieved by 6th divisional T.M's. Guns brought out.	
	5/1/17 – 25/1/17		Our guns refitting at Kent Hill. T.M Ble. at Burbure. Division in rest billets. T.M. Officers went to R.F.O, musketry and other discipline parades, etc. and instruction was given in the firing of rifle musketry etc.	
	26/1/17		Inspection by the C.R.A. – General Wellesby, who congratulated the Bde. on their good work and expressed satisfaction with their general appearance and turnout.	
	27/1/17		Prepared to move to rest billets at an hour's notice, with Bde. to Ferfay.	
	27/1/17 29/1/17		Moved with Bde to Ferfay. Oliver A. Baldwin 2nd Lt. R.F.A. comdg 1/21 T.M. Btty Moved carts Col. to Bourecq.	

T2184. Wt. W708–776. 500000. 4/15. Sir J. C. & S.

Army Form C. 2118.

WAR DIARY
or
INTELLIGENCE SUMMARY. Z 21 Trench Mortar Battery.
(Erase heading not required.)

Instructions regarding War Diaries and Intelligence Summaries are contained in F. S. Regs., Part II. and the Staff Manual respectively. Title pages will be prepared in manuscript.

Place	Date	Hour	Summary of Events and Information	Remarks and references to Appendices
	1917 January		The battery moved from the trenches to rest-billets on January 4th and carried on the usual training up to January 27th.	

W.J. Robertson Lieut
O.C. Z 21 Trench Mortar Battery.

T.M Brigade 21st Bm

WAR DIARY
INTELLIGENCE SUMMARY.

1/21. Heavy Trench Mortar Bty

For February 1919.

Vol 8

Place	Date	Hour	Summary of Events and Information	Remarks and references to Appendices

During the periods of this report there has not been much firing done owing to the Battery being out of action till 16th. From the 1st till 11th the Battery was in Billets at F.2.3½.3 (sheet 5A) on 11th we proceeded to Bethune and took over Billets at E.11.c.6.7 (sheet 36b) After remaining here 5 days one half of Battery proceeded to L.8.c.99.(") the other half proceeding to the line taking over 3 guns in the Cambrin Sector and one in the Hohenzollern Sector. Up to the end of the month A and C guns in the Cambrin Sector have shot regularly according to prearranged programme, the parts mostly affected being A28 and A22. The gun in the Hohenzollern Sector has not fired owing to the Gun Emplacement being repaired by the R.Es.

J.J.Killer
Capt. R.F.A
Comdg 1/21 HTMBty

WAR DIARY
or
INTELLIGENCE SUMMARY.

Army Form C. 2118.

Place	Date	Hour	Summary of Events and Information	Remarks and references to Appendices
	February 1917		X.21 Trench Mortar Battery. During the first part of the month the Battery, with the remainder of the Brigade, were in reserve to troops North of Ypres, being billeted at WORMHOUT. On 16th February the Battery took over the Haberg-Aken Sector from 6th Divisional Trench Mortar Battery, Headquarters at 36.e.NW.1.G.32.74. The enemy have being quiet against this front, except for firing trench mortars against well defined spots on our front. The Battery fired a minimum of 50 rounds per day, but were hindered from reaching this figure by frequent failures of the gun to act, owing to faulty R.F.T. mechanisms. On one occasion the R.F.D. mechanism had to be replaced for five shots, this being a typical example of the troubles experienced with the rifles mechanism which is frequently blown out of the gun, or the bolt jerky blown off.	
				J. B. Wignall Capt. OC X.21 Battery

WAR DIARY *or* **INTELLIGENCE SUMMARY.**
(Erase heading not required.)

Army Form C. 2118.

Y/21 T.M. Bty.

Place	Date.	Hour	Summary of Events and Information	Remarks and references to Appendices
Tenfay	1/2/17		Battery left Tenfay and travelled by road to Wormhoudt	
Wormhoudt			Battery at rest in billets at Wormhoudt. Time employed	
	2/2/17 to 11/2/17		in usual cleaning, rifle musketry inspection, and drill etc. 2/Lt O.H. Goodwin in command of the Battery.	
			Granted Temporary rank of Lieutenant.	
Battn	11/2/17 to 16/2/17		Battery in billets at Bethune, having travelled by rail from Wormhoudt on the evening of the 11th.	
A.27.c. 92.80	16/2/17 29/2/17		Battery in action in Cambrin Sector. Three guns in action on the front. About 290 rounds were fired on enemy Front Line & supports trenches and Bunter 100 rounds a day. Bty. wire defences arranged & Railway Point. The Brigadier expressed himself as pleased with the Battery's work on the Special target. A lot of trouble was experienced with rifle unknown.	

Oliver H. Goodwin
Lt. R.F.A. Y/21 T.M. Bty.

Army Form C. 2118.

WAR DIARY
or
INTELLIGENCE SUMMARY.

(Erase heading not required.)

Z 21 Trench Mortar Battery

Instructions regarding War Diaries and Intelligence Summaries are contained in F. S. Regs., Part II. and the Staff Manual respectively. Title pages will be prepared in manuscript.

Place	Date	Hour	Summary of Events and Information	Remarks and references to Appendices
MAP 36 B. N.E. L.3.	Feb 16th	6.15ᵃᵐ	Battery at rest. Usual training and inspections.	
	17th		Fired 37 rounds 2" successfully damaging German wire	
	18th		" 63 rounds in retaliation to a few German Trench Mortars.	
	19th		Fired 33 rounds on German front line doing considerable damage to his trenches.	
	20th		Fired 41 rounds on German front and support lines with excellent results.	
	21st		Fired 35 rounds on German Trenches in retaliation to a few Trench mortars.	
	22nd		Fired 87 rounds on German wire and Trenches.	
	23rd		" 48 " " "	
	24th		" 23 " " "	
			Total fired up to Feb 24th = 347	

W.B. Robertson Lieut
O.C. Z 21 Trench Mortar Battery

Army Form C. 2118.

X/21 Medium
T.M Battery

WAR DIARY
or
INTELLIGENCE SUMMARY.
(Erase heading not required.)

Place	Date	Hour	Summary of Events and Information	Remarks and references to Appendices
	March 1917.		X.21 Trench Mortar Battery. The first 3 weeks of the month were spent in action in the Hohenzollern Sector and a raid was carried out by the Infantry in connection with which wire was cut at Northern Crater. On the 21st March the Battery moved by easy stages to Arrington Wood and supplied fatigue parties to dig gun-pits for the Field Artillery.

30th March 1917.

J. Sheppard Lieut. R.F.A.
Commanding X.24 T.M. Battery | |

Army Form C. 2118.

V/21 Heavy T.M Battery
D T.M Battery
March 1917
VM 10

WAR DIARY
or
INTELLIGENCE SUMMARY.
(Erase heading not required.)

Place	Date	Hour	Summary of Events and Information	Remarks and references to Appendices
			V/21 Heavy Trench Mortar Battery at SAILLY LABOURSE	
	1/3/17		In action in Cambrin Sector	
	6/3/17			
	7/3/17		Left SAILLY for BETHUNE	
	14/3/17		Left BETHUNE for LUCHEUX	
	18/3/17		Left LUCHEUX	
	19/3/17		Arrived ARRAS	
	20/3/17		Left ARRAS } During this period the men were engaged in digging gun pits for 9th B.H.	
	26/3/17 to 31/3/17		Arrived ADINFER	

J.J.Fuller Capt
R.F.A.
O.C. V/21 H.T.M.B.A.

Y/21 Medium T.M. Battery
Y/21 T.M.Bty - March 17

WAR DIARY
INTELLIGENCE SUMMARY

Place	Date	Hour	Summary of Events and Information	Remarks
Cambrin	1/3/17		In action with two guns in Cambrin Sector. Fired about 40 rounds per gun.	
	5/3/17		About 120 rounds were expended in a special shoot on Railway Post. Much trouble with rifle mechanism.	
	6/3/17	11 a.m.	Relieved by 5th Divisional T.M.s. Returned to A.R.A. in Sailly la Bourse.	
Sailly la Bourse	6/3/17		Capt. F.K. Astin, R.F.A. relinquished the command of T.M. Bty. Capt. E.I. Davies, R.L. assumed D.T.M.O.	
	7/3/17		Battery moved to billets in Bethune - By Lorry.	
Bethune	7/3/17		Battery in billets at Bethune.	
	14/3/17		Route marches, arm drills, etc.	
	14/3/17		Battery moved by train to Lillers & thence by lorries to camp at Lucheux.	
Lucheux	19/3/17		Battery moved to Arras by lorries.	
	22/3		All O.Rs engaged on digging fatigues for 74th Bde R.F.A.	
Arras	26/3			
Achicourt	26/3		Marched to Achicourt Wood and bivouaced in the open.	
	29/3		Battery engaged on fatigues for divisional artillery - living in the open.	
	31/3			

Oliver H. Goodwin
Lt R.F.A. comdg. Y/21 T.M. Bty.

Army Form C. 2118.

WAR DIARY
or
INTELLIGENCE SUMMARY.
(Erase heading not required.)

Z 21 TRENCH MORTAR BTY

for MARCH 1917.

Place	Date	Hour	Summary of Events and Information	Remarks and references to Appendices
G.11.d.9.2	MAR. 1-6		We began the month having four guns in action but on the 6th the number was decreased to three owing to the great fatigue of the Division being relieved. During the month we fired 230 rounds on to the enemy's front & support trenches at G.12.d.5.9 G.12.d.3.1 and G.11.b.8.5 with excellent results and in addition to Minenwerfers in their dugouts emplacements.	
	6-21		Our firing was also owing to press trouble into Rifle exchanges, but 557 rounds were expended on the usual targets also via G.12.11.b G.5.d.6.3. We also piled a minenwerfer at G.12.d.4.2. We came in of action the night 21/22 March. Ammunition fired 787 rounds.	

Capt. Fisher
Maj. R.F.A.
per O.C. Z/I.T.M. Bty.

Army Form C. 2118.

V/21 Heavy Trench Mortar Battery

For April 1917

WAR DIARY
or
INTELLIGENCE SUMMARY.
(Erase heading not required.)

Place	Date	Hour	Summary of Events and Information	Remarks and references to Appendices
Map Ref France Sheet 51 B.S.W. S.29.d.	1.4.17 to 30.4.17		Supplied working Parties to 21st Divisional Artillery and 21st Divisional Ammunition Column. Lieut J.G. Harding being attached to HQ 95 Brigade RFA	
	22.4.17		Lieut L.G. Sykes was attached to 94th Brigade, and Lieut A.C. Brown to the 21st D.A.C.	
	28.4.17		Capt J.A. Tuile attached for duty with 95 Brigade RFA	

E Dark Capt G.T.
21st D.T.M.O.

Army Form C. 2118.

WAR DIARY
or
INTELLIGENCE SUMMARY.
(Erase heading not required.)

X 21 French Mortar Battery

for April 1917

Place	Date	Hour	Summary of Events and Information	Remarks and references to Appendices
Map France Sheet 51.B. SW. 3.29.d	April 1st		Supplied working parties to 21st Divisional Artillery.	
	2nd			
	3rd		Proceeded to Deas & supplied working parties to 51st Divisional Artillery.	
	4th		Lieut D. Fergusson R.F.A. was attached to 51st French Mortar Brigade	
	24th		from 4th to 10th.	
	24th		Returned to 21st Division.	
	25th		One officer and fifteen men attached to 99th Bde R.F.A.	
	6th		95th "	
	30			

W.G. Robertson Lieut
for O.C. X21 F.M. Bty.

Army Form C. 2118.

1/2[?] [?] [?] Horse Battery

For April 1917

WAR DIARY
or
INTELLIGENCE SUMMARY.
(Erase heading not required.)

Instructions regarding War Diaries and Intelligence Summaries are contained in F. S. Regs., Part II. and the Staff Manual respectively. Title pages will be prepared in manuscript.

Place	Date	Hour	Summary of Events and Information	Remarks and references to Appendices
Map Ref [?] S.29.D.	April 1st			
	2nd		Supplies working parties to 251st Divisional Artillery	
	3rd			
	4th		Provided to Ammn and supplies working parties to 51st Divisional Artillery. Lieut Loudhan RFA was attached 57th Brigade	
			Mule Bde from 4th to 10th	
	24th		Returned to 21st Division	
	21st			
	30th		All men & Officers attached to 9th Brigade RFA	

[signature]
In Ft Ypres [?]

Army Form C. 2118.

WAR DIARY
or
INTELLIGENCE SUMMARY.

(Erase heading not required.)

Z.21 French Mortar Battery

For April 1917

Vol XI

Place	Date	Hour	Summary of Events and Information	Remarks and references to Appendices
MAP Square Sht 51.B.S.W. S 29 d.	April 1st to 3rd		Supplied working parties to 21st Divisional Artillery.	
	4th to		Proceeded to Arras and supplied working parties to 21st Divisional Artillery. First Stokes R.F.A. was attached to 51st French Mortar Brigade from 4th to 10th.	
	24th		Returned to 21st Division.	
	25th to 30th		All men and one officer attached to 99th Brigade R.F.A.	

W.J. Robertson Lieut
O.C. Z.21 French Mortar Battery

Major T. M. Briggs
1/21 Heavy Trench Mortar Bty

WAR DIARY
or
INTELLIGENCE SUMMARY.
(Erase heading not required.)

Vol 12

Place	Date	Hour	Summary of Events and Information	Remarks and references to Appendices
Sgd 29	May 1st to May 31st		The personnel attached to 21st Divisional Artillery	

Abelson Capt RA
OC 1/21 H.T.M.Bty.

Army Form C. 2118.

WAR DIARY
or
INTELLIGENCE SUMMARY.
(Erase heading not required.)

X/21 Medium / Trench-mortar Battery

Instructions regarding War Diaries and Intelligence Summaries are contained in F. S. Regs., Part II. and the Staff Manual respectively. Title pages will be prepared in manuscript.

Place	Date	Hour	Summary of Events and Information	Remarks and references to Appendices
S29.d.2.9	May 2nd to May 9th		A detachment of X/21 Battery, in conjunction with detachments from Z & Y Batteries, were in action in the Hindenburg Support Line at (Map Étaing) 5¹.B.S.w.) T.6.b.4.9 on May 4th to 2nd July / and 0 7.d / and 0 12.d / Grounds on the German trench sl V.i.c.6.5 obtaining several direct hits. Retaliation from enemy artillery was heavy.	
	May 23 to May 29		Detachment dug two emplacements at 07.d.1.6 & 013.d 3.2. in Hindenberg Front line. On May 29th the detachment fired 32 rounds 3 during the 10 minutes bombardment for the Infantry attack at 1.55 p.m. Retaliation from enemy artillery was heavy.	

2nd Lt D. Stephenson
B.C. x/21 T M B Y

Army Form C. 2118.

WAR DIARY
or
INTELLIGENCE SUMMARY.   X 21 Medium Trench-mortar Battery

(Erase heading not required.)

Place	Date	Hour	Summary of Events and Information	Remarks and references to Appendices
S.29.d.2.9.	May 2nd to May 9th		A detachment of X/21 Battery, in conjunction with detachments from Z & Y Batteries, were in action in the Hindenburg Support line at (Map Etaping 51 B.S.W.) T.6.d.9.1. on May 2nd. They fired 10 rounds on the German block at V.1.C.5.5. obtaining several direct hits. Retaliation from enemy artillery was heavy. On May 3rd they fired 30 rounds during the preliminary bombardment for the Infantry attack at 3.45 p.m.	
	May 23 to May 24th		Detachments dug two emplacements in Hindenburg front line at V.7.d.1.6 and V.13.d.3.2. On May 24th the detachments fired 32 rounds during the 10 minute's bombardment in the Infantry attack at 1.55pm.	

2nd Lt. D. Septimus
O.C X/21 T.M. B⁴

Army Form C. 2118.

WAR DIARY
or
INTELLIGENCE SUMMARY.   Y/21 Medium Trench Mortar Battery
(Erase heading not required.)

Instructions regarding War Diaries and Intelligence Summaries are contained in F. S. Regs., Part II. and the Staff Manual respectively. Title pages will be prepared in manuscript.

Place	Date	Hour	Summary of Events and Information	Remarks and references to Appendices
S.29.d.2.9.	2/5/17 to 9/5/17		A detachment of Y/21 Trench Mortar Battery in conjunction with detachments from X and Z/21 T.M. Btys. were in action in the Hindenburg Support line at Tea 97 (Map Bleupiquy 51B.S.W) on May 2nd. They fired ten (10) Bombs on the German Block at U.1.c.55, obtaining several direct hits. The retaliation from enemy artillery was heavy.	
	23/5/17 to 27/5/17		A detachment formed from men drawn from X, Y and Z/21 T.M. Btys. dug two emplacements at U.9.d.16 and U.13.d.32 in Hindenburg front line. On May 27th, 32 bombs were fired from this emplacement during the 10 minutes bombardment for the Infantry attack at 1·55 p.m. Enemy retaliation was very heavy.	

R/Smellan 2nd Lt: RFA
1/6 Y/21 4th MG Bty

Army Form C. 2118.

WAR DIARY
or
INTELLIGENCE SUMMARY.   Y/21 Medium Trench Mortar Battery

(Erase heading not required.)

Place	Date	Hour	Summary of Events and Information	Remarks and references to Appendices
S.29.d 2.9	2/5/17 to 9/5/17		A detachment of Y/21 Trench Mortar Battery in conjunction with detachments from X and Z/21 T.M.B'ys were in action at T.4 & 57 (Nos. B182,B184, 51.B.S.W.) on May 2nd. They fired ten (10) Bombs on the German trench at M.c 55, obtaining several direct hits. The retaliation from enemy artillery was heavy.	
	8/5/17 to 9/5/17		T.M.B'ys dug two emplacements at U.7.a.16 and U.13.d.32 in Hindenburg Front line. On May 27th, 32 Bombs were fired from the emplacement during a 10 minutes bombardment for the Infantry attack at 1.55 pm. Enemy retaliation was very heavy.	

R Lansdown 2nd Lt. R.F.A
1/c Y/21 T.M.B'y

Army Form C. 2118.

WAR DIARY
or
INTELLIGENCE SUMMARY.   Z 21 Trench Mortar Battery

(Erase heading not required.)

Place	Date	Hour	Summary of Events and Information	Remarks and references to Appendices
S.29.d.2.9.	May 2nd to 9th		A detachment of Z 21 Mortars was in action in the Hindenburg support line at (Mg. Ebergham 51.B.s.w.) T.7.d.9.7. On May 2nd detachment fired 10 rounds on German trench at U.10.s.5. scoring several direct hits. The enemy put up what (Mg. Etergien (M.B.s.w.) was temp. Hd.Qts to his own artillery.	
	23rd to 27th		On May 3rd Detachment fired 30 rounds during preliminary bombardment before the infantry attack at 3.45 p.m. on detachments logging any movements in Hindenburg front line at U.7.d.1.6. & U.13.b.3.2. On May 27th. The detachments fired 30 rounds during the preliminary bombardment preceding the infantry attack at 10th.	

Note: The detachments from Z 21 T.M. By referred to during the month were working in conjunction with detachments from X 21 & Y 21 T.M. Bys and were working in one batty.

W.J. Robertson Lieut
O.C. Z 21 T.M. By

Army Form C. 2118.

WAR DIARY
or
INTELLIGENCE SUMMARY. Z.21 Trench Mortar Battery

(Erase heading not required.)

Place	Date	Hour	Summary of Events and Information	Remarks and references to Appendices
S.29.d.2.9.	May 1st to 9th		A detachment of Z.21 battery was in action in the Hindenburg support line at 6 On May 2nd detachment fired 11 rounds of H.E. at German trench at Hising subject to his own artillery. The enemy sent up lights. (say which paragraph they should be)	
"	23rd to 27th		On May 3rd detachment fired 30 rounds during preliminary Infantry attack at 3.45 p.m. on Hindenburg front line at U.7.d.1.1.6. detachments digging emplacements U.13.6.3.2. On May 27th the detachments fired 32 rounds during the preliminary bombardment preceding the Infantry attack at 1.55 p.m.	

Note the detachments from Z.21. T.M.Btty referred to during this month were working in conjunction with detachments from X.21 & Y.21. T.M. Btys and were working all three batteries as one battery.

W.G. Robertson Lieut
O.C. Z.21. T.M.B'y

WAR DIARY or INTELLIGENCE SUMMARY

Army Form C. 2118.

V/21 Heavy Trench Mortar 736 21st J. M. Brigade

Vol 13

Place	Date	Hour	Summary of Events and Information	Remarks and references to Appendices
U.13.a.10.5	April 17th 18th 22nd 23rd – 30th		Adtig. under orders received on June were to be made ready for action. Dugouts, trench stores & emplacement were built & gun brought up ready to open fire at M.Z.K.hn ordered viz when the Brigade had reopened this offensive. The operation being un-successful fire was not opened. Ammunition hostyr Machine gun emplacement & dump all received attention. Half-platoons of the battery were relieved by 1/25 H.T.M.B. & the personnel less half-platoon 33rd Div Adtig. after workshop position & the other half from 1/21 H.M. Camp (Corps) at x.17.c.4.5.	

Ashton CMRR
OC V/21 HTMB

WAR DIARY
or
INTELLIGENCE SUMMARY.

X, Y + Z Trench Mortar Batteries
21st June [?]

Army Form C. 2118.

	Summary of Events and Information	Remarks
	Trench Mortar Batteries acting under orders received were told [...] a special operation. Shoulrah from 28/17 [...] trench mortar rounds were fired and [...] that fire was not to be opened [...] relation to Trench Mortar [...] U7.D + U.14.A [...] garden; not being successful as fire was opened. Two guns started cutting wire which was unfavourable from any front and three + has held of the infantry in its human attack the Shoots with ordinary retaliation shooting was carried on all the 23rd Inst: When the Brigade was himself at about that time	
23	Half the Brigade went at [?] Every not amount X17C.65 + remainder proceeded working parties to the 33rd Dear Acts	

A Hedden Captn RFA
for 21st DTMO

WAR DIARY
or
INTELLIGENCE SUMMARY.

(Erase heading not required.)

1/21 Heavy Trench Mortar Batty

Army Form C. 2118.

Place	Date	Hour	Summary of Events and Information	Remarks and references to Appendices
T.18.B.8.2.	May 1st	7h	Half battery now at artillery rest camp. The remainder went into action in the line. Provided working parties for the M.T.Ms.	
	7h.12			
	2h			
	2h.5	Proceeded with the emplacements for heavy T.Ms. at O.13.a	
	3h.50			
	3h			

G.H. Gordon Capt. R.F.A.
A/ OC Heavy Trench Mortar Bty

Army Form C. 2118.

N/21 medium T M Batt

WAR DIARY
or
INTELLIGENCE SUMMARY.
(Erase heading not required.)

Place	Date	Hour	Summary of Events and Information	Remarks and references to Appendices
T.18.B.82.	JULY 1917		N/21 Trench Mortar Battery.	
			1st to 7th July. Fatigue work was done when the R.E. a coke (French) lining dug. Gun pits were dug on the BURG TRENCH front and on the 8th July the Battery came into action with 4 guns. Very exciting was done preparatory to RAIDS by the Infantry. For this purpose the Battery shot in cooperation with 18 pdrs, the latter covering n all known enemy C.P.S. and on intervals. By this fire covering n the Infantry on the enemy trenches.	
			The Battery was prepared to retaliate n enemy T.M. fire but no enemy T.M. fires with exception of 20 or 30 aerial darts on the centre of the sump	

J. Whippersheim Major
Cmdg. N21 T.M. Battery

WAR DIARY
INTELLIGENCE SUMMARY

Army Form C. 2118.

July 1917.

1/3rd Medium Trench Mortar Battery

Place	Date	Hour	Summary of Events and Information	Remarks and references to Appendices
T.18.B.82	1st to 7th		Supplied fatigue parties to the R.E's to dig a cable trench	
	8th to 14th		Gun Emplacements were started on the HINDENBURG FRONT LINE and guns were taken into action	
	15th to 31st		In conjunction with Divnl Artillery several shoots were successfully carried out. Target Enemy wire and Trenches. Work was also done on positions and dugouts.	

S. Davis Capt.
O.C. M.T.B.

WAR DIARY
or
INTELLIGENCE SUMMARY

Army Form C. 2118.

7/2/ Medium Trench Mortar Battery

Place	Date	Hour	Summary of Events and Information	Remarks and references to Appendices
7.18.B.8.2	9 to 14 July		The battery was split up, one half going to rest at HENDECOURT and the other was occupied in digging gun pits in the HINDENBURG FRONT LINE.	
	20.7.17	3 P.M.	The enemy front line was bombarded and wire cut at U14.a.37 and U14.a.0580 (CHERISY 1:10000 map). Observation was difficult as no O.P. could be found near the gun. In all 190 bombs were fired, the bombardment lasting one hour.	
	23.7.17.	7 P.M.	Enemy wire bombarded at U14.a.0575. 30 bombs were fired and a small gap cut.	
	24.7.17	12 Noon	16 bombs were fired to increase damage done to wire the previous day.	
	26.7.17	5 pm	19 bombs were fired at M.G. emplacement at U11.c.18 and wire. Two gaps have been cut. At 6 pm 6 more bombs were fired.	
	24/25 7/17	6 P.M. 2.50 a.m.	On the night of 24/25 July we fired 112 bombs in support of an infantry raiding party. Work has been carried on all the time improving the pits and bomb stores.	

Llewellyn
OC 7/2 M.T.M.B.

WAR DIARY
INTELLIGENCE SUMMARY

V/21 Heavy Trench Mortar Bty, Army Form C. 2118
21st T.M Brigade

Vol 15

Place	Date	Hour	Summary of Events and Information	Remarks and references to Appendices
18.B.74	6.9.17 13.9.17		Work on continued in new emplacement.	
	14th		Relieved new piece from no 4 position of Oldham Caw. & Trench Mortar down 6.7.D	
	16th 23rd		Eg.N/W between new emplacements at same hour – no direct damage was done. Forty five rounds were fired at selected targets in Zandvoorde (V.9.B.4.2) receives special attention.	
	3rd		Many rounds fired, heavy new batteries and 6 pdr. Trench Mortar Brun – trench kund Julin, Fry Alley, trench &	
	31st		Battery relieved by incoming division & taken out to a short rest.	

A.J.Nelson Capt R.F.A
O.C. V/21 H.T.M.B

WAR DIARY or INTELLIGENCE SUMMARY

Army Form C. 2118.

X/21 Trench Mortar By. August, 1917.

Place	Date	Hour	Summary of Events and Information	Remarks and references to Appendices
T.18.B.74	1st/10 14th		During this period the Battery attended a course of instruction on the 6 inch trench Howitzer at the Third Army T.M. School and obtained efficiency in drill and firing of this new weapon.	
	15th/10		Battery took over from 58th T.M.B. Enemy fire was slight, consequently retaliation was only called for on 3 or 4 occasions, 5 or 6 Rounds being fired each time.	
	16th			
	17th/10 30th		Three Special Shoots were carried out on 17th, 23rd and 29th in conjunction with Artillery. Target Enemy wire and trenches. Retaliation was very slight on these occasions.	
	31st		Battery relieved by X/16 T.M. By and tuckon out to rest	

A. Wilson
Capt.
O.C. X/21 T.M.By.

WAR DIARY or INTELLIGENCE SUMMARY

Army Form C. 2118.

1/2¹ Medium Trench Mortar Battery
BEF FRANCE
AUGUST 1917

Place	Date	Hour	Summary of Events and Information	Remarks and references to Appendices
T.18.B.1.4. (P.3)	1.8.17		The work of digging the new emplacements next to guns in action it had been completed in the previous month	
		2.30 PM	Each was done during August by Infantry working dugouts. We have our almost finished the work being done many by the two medium batteries of the 58th Div attached to this Division. Also reserve position were started, this being under the influence of a star of Division	
		3 PM	The shooting consisted in a continued effort of 1 & 2 Batteries. Each took at 2.30 or 3 PM 50 rounds, the gun would fire over to destroy enemy wire. The 1 & 2 H Battery covered in fire very little retaliation on part of the Boche. This is of time objects were successfully carried out. We had taken over another battery from the 7th Division on our right (J.14) about the beginning of the month, which was worked by one of the attached 58th Division owing to the absence of our own X Battery being on a fortnight course at the 3rd Army Trench Mortar School in the new 6" Newton Gun, which	
	14.8.17		course was over by Aug 14. On their return, X Battery personnel	

WAR DIARY or INTELLIGENCE SUMMARY

Y/21 MEDIUM TRENCH MORTAR BATTERY
BEF FRANCE
AUGUST 1917

Place	Date	Hour	Summary of Events and Information Continued (2)	Remarks and references to Appendices
(Y.14)	14/8/17 17/8/17		relieved the 58th Div. battery. Owing to lack of officers to Y Battery officer in the line was responsible for both X and Y Batteries. Whilst this new arrangement we had two more similar shafts always on entering were with occasional revisits in the front line and trench junctions. This time were were further substantiated by the Heavy T.M's being first	
	19.8.17	2.30PM	Shoot X Battery had 3 guns in action. Y Battery had 3 guns firing each. The no 4 gun of X Battery for a direct hit (bullseye) necessitating the building of new emplacement. Second shoot the guns on not out of action during the work of new position. Were launched enough to hold	
	30.8.17	2.30 PM	the condition of the Trench system. On the X Battery front the "HUMP" (so-called) was extremely bad owing to the fierce nature of the shell fire and Trench Mortar fire in that Sector.	
			Y Battery had one gun in action for S.O.S purposes, & firing always best furnished but that gun. (No.1)	

A. Cosher Lieut
A/Sherwood Foresters
Comm'g Y/21 M. T. M. B

WAR DIARY

Army Form C. 2118.

2/21 Medium Trench Mortar Battery

INTELLIGENCE SUMMARY.

(Erase heading not required.)

Place	Date	Hour	Summary of Events and Information	Remarks and references to Appendices
7.18.B.7d	6.8.17	5pm	Three (3) bombs were fired at enemy line at U7d.45.80. A dugout was started being No 4 gun (U7d.00.58)	Map reference to BULLECOURT
	10.8.17		A new position was started about U7c.90.60	
	12.8.17	3pm	Three (3) ranging bombs were fired from No 3 Gun at enemy were at U7d.50.75.	Map reference
	14.8.17	3p.m.	74 bombs were fired at enemy fire from U7b.35.00 to U7d.60.20 and the strong point at U7b.45.20, much damage being done	No 1 Gun fd's U7d.00.58 No 2 – U7d.05.10
	15.8.17	4pm	76 bombs were fired from No 4 gun (U7c.00.58) for registration	No 2 – U7d.50.30 U7d.05.30
	17.8.17	7.45pm	Nine (9) bombs were fired at enemy who were at U7d.50.30 and a small gap cut through the enemy retaliation was very heavy on white lights going up from his front line.	No 3 – U7d.00.48 No 4 – U7d.00.58
	18.8.17	4.30pm	At the request of the battery on the right 9 fired 12 rounds to cover heavy fire. The shooting was poor owing to a head wind which was blowing in squalls. A great deal of work was put in at new position and in finishing the dugout at No 4 Gun which should do for four men	

7.18.17
17.8.17

WAR DIARY
of
INTELLIGENCE SUMMARY.
(Erase heading not required.)

2/2 M.T.M.B. Army Form C. 2118.

Part II. 2

Place	Date	Hour	Summary of Events and Information	Remarks and references to Appendices
	22/8/17	2:30 pm	The enemy front line and wire was bombarded with good results. Gaps were cut in the wire in several places between U7d 6025 and U7d 6595. A saphead with loophole was hit and much damage done to the enemy front line. 105 bombs were fired. No 2 gun was hit and a slight fire caused but no damage done to the gun or bombs. The retaliation was slight.	
	30/8/17	3 pm	The enemy strong point at U7b 4020 was again bombarded and the wire round it cut. Prime Trench received several direct hits about U7b 5025. This shoot was in conjunction with the 9.45 T.M. The damage done was very great both to the wire and front line (Fire on by Nos 3 & 4 Guns) — No 1 gun cut the enemy wire at U7d 6530 and No 2 cut gaps at U7d 5050.	
	31/8/17		Battery was relieved by 2/16 T.M. Bty.	

D Howclaw 2/Lieut
O.C. 2/2 M.T.M.B.
7/9
Signed R.F.A.

Army Form C. 2118.

WAR DIARY
or
INTELLIGENCE SUMMARY.
(Erase heading not required.)

V/121)
X/121) Trench Mortar Batteries
Y/121)
Z/121)

9/C/16

Instructions regarding War Diaries and Intelligence Summaries are contained in F. S. Regs., Part II. and the Staff Manual respectively. Title pages will be prepared in manuscript.

Place	Date	Hour	Summary of Events and Information	Remarks and references to Appendices
Map Belgium & France Sheet 28 H.32.d.5.1.	Sept 1st		Batteries at rest	
	6th		Proceeded to Godewaersvelde	
	6th		Proceeded to H.32.d.5.1.	
	13th		Supplied working parties to 39th, 41st & 21st Div. Artillerie	
	18/9			
	6th		Supplied reinforcements to 21st Div. Arty.	
	20th			

W.B. Robertson Lieut
for D.T.M.O.

WAR DIARY or INTELLIGENCE SUMMARY

V, X, Y, & Z/21 Trench Mortar Batteries

Army Form C. 2118.

Place	Date	Hour	Summary of Events and Information	Remarks and references to Appendices
Sht 28. H.32.d.5.1.	1917 Oct.		Personnel (Officers & O.R.) of V, X, Y, & Z/21 Trench Mortar Batteries were attached to 94th & 95th Brigades R.F.A. as reinforcements	

W.A. Robertson Lt.
for 21st D.T.M.O.

WAR DIARY V/21, X/21, Y/21 & Z/21 Army Form C. 2118.
or
INTELLIGENCE SUMMARY. Trench Mortar Batteries

Place	Date	Hour	Summary of Events and Information	Remarks and references to Appendices
Ref. Map 1/20,000 51B.N.W. H.1.c.28.	Nov. 1st to 13th		Personnel of V, X, Y, & Z batteries were attached to 94th & 95th Bdes R.F.A as reinforcements.	
	15th to 20th		Batteries on the line of march from 3rd Army to 1st Army	
	21st		X, Y & Z batteries in action in the trenches. V battery supplied working parties in the trenches.	
	22nd to 27th		Working on new gun positions for 6" Newton French Mortars. Fired 33 rounds 6" Newton T.M.S	
	Dec.26th		20 O.R. of V/21 T.M.Bty were attached to 176th Tunnelling Coy. R.E. for work in trenches.	

W.I. Robertson Lt.
No 21 D.T.M.O.

WAR DIARY or INTELLIGENCE SUMMARY

Army Form C. 2118.

X/21 ⎫
Y/21 ⎬ Trench Mortar Batteries
Z/21 ⎭

Dec 1917

Y 19

Milne? Right RFA
D.T.M.O. 21st DIVISION.

Place	Date	Hour	Summary of Events and Information	Remarks
	December 1917			
	1st		Left ROCLINCOURT and proceeded to BEAULENCOURT.	
	2nd		Proceeded to BRUSLE	
	4th to 12th		Supplied 30 Other Ranks to work on an Ammunition Dump at Y 19 siding.	
	8th		Proceeded to TINCOURT WOOD.	
	14th		4 Officers and 40 Other Ranks proceeded to the 5th Army Trench Mortar School, to attend a course of instruction in the 6" Mortar.	

WAR DIARY
or
INTELLIGENCE SUMMARY.

Army Form C. 2118.

X/21 }
Y/21 } Trench Mortar Batteries
Z/21 }

Vol 20

Place	Date	Hour	Summary of Events and Information	Remarks and references to Appendices
	JANUARY 1918			
	5		Left TINCOURT WOOD and proceeded to LIERAMONT.	
	13		Left LIERAMONT and proceeded to DRIENCOURT.	
	16		2 Officers and 25 Other Ranks proceeded to EPEHY in order to construct defensive Trench Mortar positions in the line	
	21		Working party in the line, increased to 2 Officers and 42 Other Ranks.	
	24		4 — 6" NEWTON Trench Mortars placed in Action, in defensive positions in the line	

Signed _____ CAPT. R.F.A.
D.T.M.O.
21ST DIVISIONAL ARTILLERY.

WAR DIARY
or
INTELLIGENCE SUMMARY.

(Erase heading not required.) X/21 & Y/21 Trench Mortar Batteries

Army Form C. 2118.

Vol 21

Place	Date	Hour	Summary of Events and Information	Remarks and references to Appendices
	February			
	3rd		Working Party of 2 Officers and 42 Other ranks withdrawn from the line to ORLENCOURT	
	12th		X/21 & Y/21 TM Batteries moved to SAULCOURT.	
	16th to 23rd		1 Officer and 30 Other ranks employed on Fatigues for Horse standings of 94th Brigade RFA.	

[signature] CAPT. R.F.A.
D.T.M.O.
21ST DIVISIONAL ARTILLERY.

Army Form C. 2118.

WAR DIARY
or
INTELLIGENCE SUMMARY.
(Erase heading not required)

21st TRENCH MORTAR BRIGADE

Place	Date	Hour	Summary of Events and Information	Remarks and references to Appendices
MARCH 1918				
	1-3-18 to 7-3-18		16 O.R. supplied for Fatigue for Head Qrs. 21st Division Artillery.	
	3-3-18		T.M.B. took over Defensive positions from 16th & 39th Div. T.M.B.	
	4-3-18 to 14-3-18		20 O.R. supplied to 126 Field Coy. R.E. to work on Construction of O.P. in EPEHY. 4 ... 6" T.M. in Action.	
	6-3-18		Two HOTCHKISS Anti Tank Guns taken over from 39th Division & placed in Action.	
	8-3-18 to 19-3-18		Anti Tank Minefield constructed. 4,370 2" T.M. Bombs placed in position & Fuzed.	
	10-3-18		Number of 6" T.M. in Action, in Defensive positions, increased to 10.	
	21-3-18		70 Rounds of 6" T.M. fired in Defence of the RED LINE 4 ... 6" T.M. & 2 HOTCHKISS Anti Tank Guns captured by Enemy.	
	22-3-18		Withdrew from EPEHY. 8. 6" T.M. captured by Enemy. 5 Hub. killed by shell fire. 3 Hub Carts & 1 water Cart captured by Enemy. Moved to HAUT ALLAINES. Moved to LONGAVESNES.	
	23-3-18		T.M.B. moved to CLERY-SUR-SOMME — 3 Hub Carts captured by Enemy - TMB moved to MARICOURT	
	24-3-18		" " BRAY.	
	25-3-18		" " ETINEHEM	
	26-3-18		" " DAOURS	
	27-3-18		" " CONTAY — 1 Officer & 40 O.R. attached to 94th Brigade RFA	
			" " " 1 " 20 " " " 95th "	
	28-3-18		12 O.R. supplied for work on Ammunition Dump at CONTAY. TMB moved to BAVELINCOURT	
	30-3-18		TMB moved to BEAUCOURT	

M. [signature] CAPT. R.F.A.
D.T.M.O.
21ST DIVISIONAL ARTILLERY.

21st Divisional Artillery.

21st DIVISIONAL TRENCH MORTAR BRIGADE

APRIL 1918.

Army Form C. 2118.

WAR DIARY
or
INTELLIGENCE SUMMARY.

(Erase heading not required.) 21ST TRENCH MORTAR BRIGADE

Instructions regarding War Diaries and Intelligence Summaries are contained in F. S. Regs., Part II. and the Staff Manual respectively. Title pages will be prepared in manuscript.

WA 23

Place	Date	Hour	Summary of Events and Information	Remarks and references to Appendices
APRIL 1918.				
	1-4-18		TMB at BEAUCOURT.	
	2-4-18		TMB Moved to Farm near MONTIGNY CHATEAU.	
	7-4-18 To 9-4-18		13 Other Ranks worked on Ammunition Dump, under 4th Australian Division Artillery	
	11-4-18		TMB moved to QUERRIEU.	
	12-4-18		TMB moved to HEM.	
	13-4-18		TMB moved to DOULLONS STATION, and enrailed in cattle trucks for 20t Div Ammn Column	
	14-4-18		TMB entrained for HOPOUTRE & marched from there to a Farm near ABEELE	
	15-4-18 To 19-4-18		Supplied 20 Other Ranks for work on Ammunition Dump, under 21st Div. Artillery.	
	18-4-18		TMB Moved to EECKE	
	20-4-18		2 & 6th Ranks attached to 95th Brigade RFA.	

Signed
CAPT. R.F.A.
D.T.M.O.
21ST DIVISIONAL ARTILLERY.

Army Form C. 2118.

WAR DIARY
or
INTELLIGENCE SUMMARY.
(Erase heading not required)

21st TRENCH MORTAR BRIGADE

Vol 24

Instructions regarding War Diaries and Intelligence Summaries are contained in F. S. Regs., Part II. and the Staff Manual respectively. Title pages will be prepared in manuscript.

Place	Date	Hour	Summary of Events and Information	Remarks and references to Appendices
	5 - 5 - 18		T.M.B. entrained at WIZERNES.	
	6 - 5 - 18		T.M.B. detrained at BOULEUSE and marched to ST GEMME.	
	14 - 5 - 18		T.M.B. moved to CHATEAU DU BOIS DE L'ARBRE.	
	21 - 5 - 18		T.M personnel attached to RFA Brigades, rejoined TM Brigade. Received 12 ..... 6" T.M. from DADOS 21st Division.	
	24 - 5 - 18		Started work on 12 ..... 6" T.M emplacements in the line.	
	27 - 5 - 18		Withdrew working parties from the line. T.M.B. marched to VANDEUIL.	
	28 - 5 - 18		T.M.B. marched to ST EUPHRAISE.	
	29 - 5 - 18		T.M.B. marched to LA NEUVILLE. 34 Other Ranks attached to 94th Brigade RFA. 32 Other Ranks attached to 95th Brigade RFA. T.M.B. moved to NANTEUIL. Handed over 12 ..... 6" T.M. to Ordnance IX Corps.	
	30 - 5 - 18		T.M.B. moved to VAUCIENNES.	

N. Noel .... CAPT. R.F.A.
D.T.M.O.
21st DIVISIONAL ARTILLERY.

Army Form C. 2118.

WAR DIARY
or
INTELLIGENCE SUMMARY.
(Erase heading not required.)

21st Trench Mortar Brigade Vol 25

Place	Date	Hour	Summary of Events and Information	Remarks and references to Appendices
JUNE 1918.	June 1918			
	15-6-18		TMB marched to VOIPREUX	
	16-6-18		" " " NORMÉE	
	19-6-18		" entrained at MAILY LE CAMP.	
	20-6-18		" detrained at PONT RUMY & marched to LIERCOURT.	
	21-6-18		" Marched to WATTEBLERY.	
	22-6-18		" " " MESNIL VAL	
	28-6-18		Received 9 6" Trench Mortars.	
	30-6-18		TMB marched to WATTEBLERY.	

D.T.M.O.
21st DIVISIONAL ARTILLERY.

CAPT. R.F.A.

Army Form C. 2118.

WAR DIARY
or
INTELLIGENCE SUMMARY.
(Erase heading not required.)

21st Trench Mortar Brigade   Vol 26

Place	Date	Hour	Summary of Events and Information	Remarks and references to Appendices
July 1918.				
July	4th – 16th		D.T.M.O. supervised training of the 3" Stokes Mortar Batteries of 21st Division	
"	21st		T.M.B. moved by lorries to BEAUQUESNE.	
"	24th		T.M.B. personnel, who were attached to A.F.A. Brigades, rejoined T.M. Brigade.	
"	26th		Took over 12 Mortars, in the line, from 63rd (R.N.) Divisional Artillery.	
"	28th		Head Qrs. 21st T.M Brigade moved to bivouacs in P16A, near ACHEUX.	
"			Head Qrs 21st T.M Brigade moved to ACHEUX.	

CAPT. R.F.A.
D.T.M.O.
21ST DIVISIONAL ARTILLERY.

Army Form C. 2118.

WAR DIARY
or
INTELLIGENCE SUMMARY.
(Erase heading not required.)

21st T.M. Brigade   Page 1.

Instructions regarding War Diaries and Intelligence Summaries are contained in F. S. Regs., Part II. and the Staff Manual respectively. Title pages will be prepared in manuscript.

Place	Date	Hour	Summary of Events and Information	Remarks and references to Appendices
ACHEUX (July 26") August 1918	1st		X/163 T.M.Bÿ came under command of D.T.M.O. Ordinary harassing and retaliating fire commenced by X/21, Y/21 & X/163 T.M.Btys. ammunition expended 79 rounds 6" Newton	
	2.1		74	
	3.1		74	
	4.1		78	
	5.1		30	
	6.1		73	
	7.1		30 X/163 T.M.By.	
	8.1		X/163 T.M.By. placed under X/163 T.M.By. Harassing fire increased. Expenditure 1,234 rounds	
	9.1		Chanak Fire 188 rounds	
	10.1		244 "	
	11.1		321 "	
	12.1		349 "	
	13.1		344 "	
	14.1		330 "	
	15.1		100 " Orders were issued to cease fire about midday as the enemy were retreating from the Beaumont Hamel ridge D.T.M.O. accompanied me for two further These could not be obtained as the range to enemy opening out for T.M. Collated from material collected of futile uses off T.M.O. attached to 99th H.A. X/163 M. came under orders of D.T.M.O. 38th Div.	W.P.Robertson Capt. actg/D.T.M.O. 21st Div.

Page 2.

Army Form C. 2118.

WAR DIARY
or
INTELLIGENCE SUMMARY.

(Erase heading not required.)

21st T.M. Brigade

Place	Date	Hour	Summary of Events and Information	Remarks and references to Appendices
AUGUST				
Mailly-Maillet	25th		Brigade moved to Mailly-Maillet 9.7.a. central.	
	26th		Received 1 mobile 6" Trench Mortar from V Corps. T.M.O.	
	27th		2 Offrs and 16 O.R's attached with mobile trench mortar to 62nd Inf. Bde.	
			54 O.R's attached to S.A.A. section 21st D.A.C.	

W.J. Robertson Capt.
acting/D.T.M.O. 21st Bde

Army Form C. 2118.

WAR DIARY
or
INTELLIGENCE SUMMARY.
(Erase heading not required.)   21st Trench Mortar Brigade

Instructions regarding War Diaries and Intelligence Summaries are contained in F. S. Regs. Part II. and the Staff Manual respectively. Title pages will be prepared in manuscript.

Place September 1918	Date	Hour	Summary of Events and Information	Remarks and references to Appendices
	1 – 9 – 18		1 Mobile 6" Mortar attached to 110th Infantry Brigade	W/D 28
	2 – 9 – 18		T.M. Brigade moved to near LE SARS	
	5 – 9 – 18		T.M. Brigade moved to near MORVAL	
	6 – 9 – 18		1 Mobile 6" Mortar attached to 62nd Infantry Brigade	
	7 – 9 – 18		T.M. Brigade moved to VAUX WOOD near MANANCOURT	
	10 – 9 – 18		T.M. Brigade moved to EQUANCOURT	
	14 – 9 – 18		Began the construction of Nine 6" Mortar emplacements near REVELON	
	18 – 9 – 18		Nine 6" Mortars cooperated with Artillery Barrage of 17th Division. -- 172 Rounds fired on enemy front line	
			1 Mobile 6" Mortar moved forward with 64th Infantry Brigade & fired 12 rounds on Machine Gun emplacements in VILLERS GUISLAIN	
	18 – 6 – 19 – 9 – 18		Personnel of T.M. Brigade assisted in removal of captured 4.2" Howitzers	
	20 – 9 – 18		Two 6" Mortars placed in reserve position, in case of enemy Counter attack	
			One Mobile Mortar attached to 19th Infantry Brigade	
	23 – 9 – 18		T.M. Brigade moved to Bivouac on EQUANCOURT – NEUVILLE ROAD	
	24 – 9 – 18		Began the Construction of Six 6" Mortar emplacements in front of CHAPEL HILL ~~to cooperate with~~ 33rd Division	
	25 – 9 – 18		Six 6" Mortars taken up to emplacements by Night by a supply Tank	
	26 – 9 – 18		One Mobile Mortar attached to 98th Infantry Brigade	
	27 – 9 – 18		Work completed on Six 6" Mortar emplacements in front of CHAPEL HILL, and ammunition brought up to them	
	29 – 9 – 18		Fired 104 rounds in cooperation with Barrage of 33rd Divisional Artillery	
			Detachments afterwards shot by Mortars, in case of enemy Counter attack.	
			Mobile Mortar attached to 98th Infantry Brigade fired 20 rounds	
			T.M. personnel fired about 250 rounds on selected targets, from captured 77mm Gun	
	30 – 9 – 18		T.M. Brigade moved to Sunken Road, near VAUCELETTE FARM	

Allard Capt. RFA
D.T.M.O. 21st DIVISION

vol 29

C O N F I D E N T I A L.

WAR DIARY

21st Trench Mortar Brigade RFA.

October 1st - 31st 1918.

Army Form C. 2118.

WAR DIARY
or
INTELLIGENCE SUMMARY.
(Erase heading not required.)

21st Trench Mortar Brigade

Instructions regarding War Diaries and Intelligence Summaries are contained in F. S. Regs., Part II. and the Staff Manual respectively. Title pages will be prepared in manuscript.

Place	Date	Hour	Summary of Events and Information	Remarks and references to Appendices
	OCTOBER 1918			
	1 — 10 — 18		TM Bde moved to near VILLERS GUISLAIN. 20 rounds from Mobile Mortar, fired on enemy Machine Gun emplacements.	
	3 — 10 — 18		Six 6" T.M.'s placed in Action, under 33rd Divisional Artillery.	
	5 — 10 — 18		One Mobile Mortar attached to 64th Inf. Brigade.	
	7 — 10 — 18		Two Mobile Mortars (in all) attached to 64th Inf. Brigade.	
	9 — 10 — 18		TM Bde moved to VAUCELLES WOOD, near BANTOUZELLE.	
	10 — 10 — 18		TM Bde moved to WALINCOURT.	
	13 — 10 — 18		Two Mobile Mortars attached to 17th TM Bde.	
	22 — 10 — 18		Two Mobile Mortars rejoined from 17th TM Bde; having fired 200 rounds in action in NEUVILLY.	
			TM Bde moved to AUDENCOURT.	
	23 — 10 — 18		TM Bde moved to NEUVILLY; 3 Mobile Mortars attached to 94th Bde RFA.	
	24 — 10 — 18		2 other Ranks attached to C/94 Bde RFA.	
			3 Mobile Mortars withdrawn from 94th Bde RFA and attached to 95th Bde RFA.	
			TM Bde moved to OVILLERS.	
	25 — 10 — 18		TM Bde moved to VENDEGIES-AU-BOIS; 3 Mobile Mortars withdrawn from 95th Bde RFA.	
	29 — 10 — 18		3 Mobile Mortars moved up to POIX-DU-NORD and kept in readiness for work with forward Battalions of 21st Division.	

_____ CAPT. R.F.A.
D.T.M.O.
21st DIVISIONAL ARTILLERY.

CONFIDENTIAL.

WAR DIARY

OF

21st Trench Mortar Brigade R.F.A.

FROM 1st November 1918. TO 30th November 1918.

Army Form C. 2118.

WAR DIARY
or
INTELLIGENCE SUMMARY.
(Erase heading not required.)

21st TRENCH MORTAR BRIGADE

Place	Date	Hour	Summary of Events and Information	Remarks and references to Appendices
NOVEMBER	4—11—18		4 Mobile Trench Mortars attached to 62nd Infantry Brigade.	
	5—11—18		T M Bde moved to LOC Q A I G N o 1	
	6—11—18		4 Mobile Trench Mortars attached to 110th Inf. Brigade & moved up to BERLAIMONT	
	7—11—18		TM Bde moved to BERLAIMONT & Mobile Trench Mortars came out of Action	
	14—11—18		Trench Mortar Ammunition dumped at AULNOYE.	
	15—11—18		T.M. Bde moved to MONTAY.	
	30—11—18		3 Mobile Mortar carriages and beds drawn from 3rd Army Gun Park	

CAPT. R.F.A.
D.T.M.O.
21st DIVISIONAL ARTILLERY.

C O N F I D E N T I A L.

WAR DIARY

OF

21st Trench Mortar Brigade R.F.A.

FROM:- December 1st.   TO:- December 31st 1918.

Army Form C. 2118.

WAR DIARY
or
INTELLIGENCE SUMMARY.
(Erase heading not required.) 21st TRENCH MORTAR BRIGADE

Place	Date	Hour	Summary of Events and Information	Remarks and references to Appendices
DECEMBER 1918	13-12-18		Mounted portion of TMB proceeded to TIRANCOURT, by Road.	
	17-12-18		Dismounted portion of TMB proceeded to INCHY, by Road.	
	19-12-18		Dismounted portion of TMB proceeded to TIRANCOURT, by Motor Transport.	

[signature] CAPT. R.F.A.
D.T.M.O.
21ST DIVISIONAL ARTILLERY.

www.ingramcontent.com/pod-product-compliance
Lightning Source LLC
Chambersburg PA
CBHW081543160426
43191CB00011B/1825